Author: Alastair Matchett

Proofreader: Andrea Ward

Content Review: Andrea Ward

Published by Adkins & Matchett (UK) Limited – trading as Adkins, Matchett & Toy

Second edition 2007

UK COPYRIGHT NOTICE

Manufactured in United Kingdom

ISBN: 978-1-891112-72-0

To order call: +44 (0) 1295 256 161 or +1 914 944 0999
Visit us at or buy online: www.amttraining.com

UK
Linden House, 55 South Bar
Banbury
Oxfordshire
OX16 9AB UK

T +44 (0) 1295 256 161
F +44 (0) 1295 272 108
E info@amttraining.com
W www.amttraining.com

USA
235 Eastern Avenue
Ossining
New York
10562 USA

T +1 914 944 0999
F +1 914 944 0465
E info@amttraining.com
W www.amttraining.com

Table of Contents

Valuation Road Map

INTRODUCTION

Valuation is fundamental to nearly every aspect of finance. In almost every finance role, you will need some understanding of valuation principles and methods. Valuation is very important in all of the following situations:

- Stand alone valuations of companies/subsidiaries
  - Mergers
  - Acquisitions
  - Company sales
  - Subsidiary sales
  - Start-ups
  - Joint ventures
  - De-listing (taking private)
  - Implementation of share option programs

- Public equity offerings: Equity offerings can be either "primary", i.e. injection/issue of new capital, or "secondary", i.e. sale by an existing shareholder. In the event of a primary share offering, the distinction between "pre-money" and "post-money" valuation is important.
  - Initial Public Offerings (IPOs)
  - Subsidiary IPOs
  - Spin-offs

- Financing
  - Re-capitalization
  - Re-structuring
  - Leveraged buyouts (LBOs)
  - Share repurchase programs

Guess what! There is no one right way to value a firm. The three most common approaches are:

- Transaction multiples
- Trading multiples
- Discounted Cash Flow (DCF)

In addition, you might encounter these methods:

- Dividend Discount Model (DDM) used for financial institutions or investment vehicles
- Leveraged value (used for leveraged buyouts)
- Breakup value or "sum-of-the-parts" value

Using a number of different methods will often give you a broad valuation range. A critical part of the analyst's role is to understand the different approaches and why you get different answers.

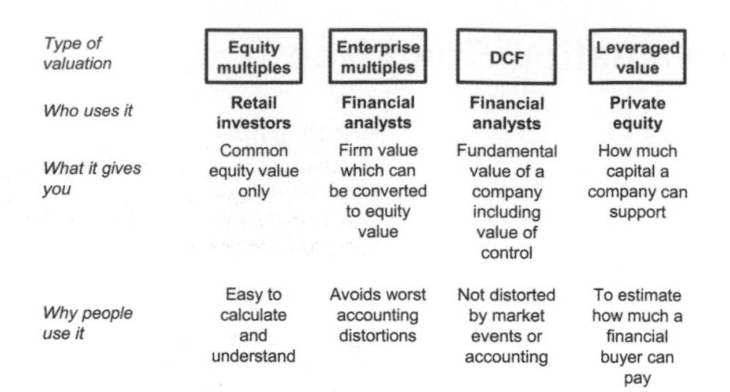

Type of valuation	Equity multiples	Enterprise multiples	DCF	Leveraged value
Who uses it	Retail investors	Financial analysts	Financial analysts	Private equity
What it gives you	Common equity value only	Firm value which can be converted to equity value	Fundamental value of a company including value of control	How much capital a company can support
Why people use it	Easy to calculate and understand	Avoids worst accounting distortions	Not distorted by market events or accounting	To estimate how much a financial buyer can pay

THE FOUNDATION

Let's start with a normal balance sheet you might find in a company's financial statements. Think of it as the accounting balance sheet. The accounting balance sheet will help you to understand the relationship between Equity Value and Enterprise Value or Firm Value.

Excess Cash Means...

Remaining assets after operational needs are met

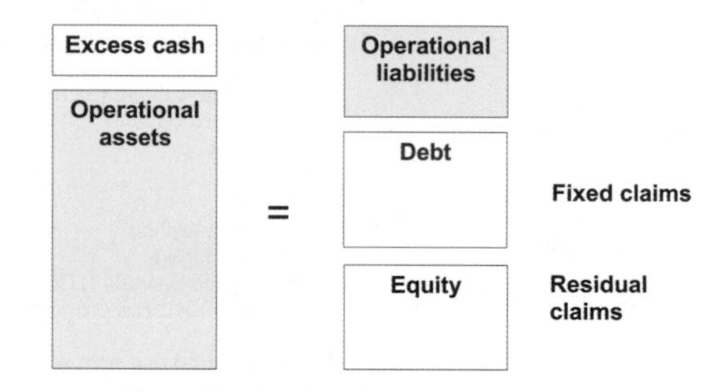

FUNDAMENTAL DIFFERENCE BETWEEN THE BLUE BLOCKS AND THE WHITE BLOCKS

Blue = Assets and liabilities driven by everyday strategic, operational and investing decisions. For example, making a sale to a customer or investing in plant and machinery.

White = Assets and liabilities determined by a company's financial strategy.

The white blocks on the right, Debt and Equity, represent the company's capital.

Company activities dictate most of the change in operational accounts. The company's financial strategy controls the white blocks.

FIXED VS. RESIDUAL CLAIMS

Debt

Debt capital represents the fixed claims against a company's assets. The company cannot NOT pay these claims, or they are in big trouble. In most situations, apart from financial restructurings, valuing debt is relatively easy as its claim against the company's assets remains fixed or constant.

Equity

Equity capital represents residual claims on a company's assets. It gets everything remaining after the debt holders are paid off. Valuing equity is more challenging as its claim against the company's assets is residual. Every time the value of the company's assets change so does the value of the equity.

Credit Nerds

People in credit have a relatively conservative view of the world. They use accounting equity value in most ratios. If a company is in financial distress, its future earnings may be in question and the value of its intangible assets like brand names will dwindle!

MARKET VALUE VS. ACCOUNTING VALUES

So far you have been looking at accounting values. Accounting is not used to value a business. Accounting tells you how a business has performed historically over a specific period and the status of its balance sheet at one moment in time. You need to make some adjustments to the accounting model to establish the company's market value.

ACCOUNTING VALUE OF EQUITY

The balance sheet equity reflects the capital invested in the business plus retained profits built up over time. Accounting equity value is also known as "book value".

MARKET VALUE OF EQUITY

Market value of equity = accounting value of equity plus:

1. Perceived value of any intangible assets not specified on the balance sheet or "goodwill"

   - Quality of management employees
   - Brand equity
   - Client relationships

2. Today's value of expected future earnings or cash flows

If a company has generated a positive historical return on equity and you compare a company's value in its equity accounts with the value of its stock in the stock market (market value), the market value should be higher.

Example - Tootsie Roll

Tootsie Roll's shareholders' equity accounts at December 31 show a value of $527m

SHAREHOLDERS' EQUITY (in thousands)	
Common stock, $.6944 par value- 120,000 shares authorized 34,248 issued......................	23,783
Class B common stock, $.6944 par value- 40,000 shares authorized 16,759 issued......................	11,638
Capital in excess of par value.............................	355,658
Retained earnings, per accompanying statement....	148,705
Accumulated other comprehensive earnings	(11,052)
Treasury stock (at cost) 55 shares	(1,992)
	526,740
	$646,080

On the same day as the annual report was filed the share price of Tootsie Roll was $30.68, equivalent to a market value of $1,563m.

RESTATING THE BALANCE SHEET USING MARKET VALUES

In order to restate the balance sheet relationships using market values, add the value of the off-balance sheet intangible assets and future growth opportunities to the asset side.

In order to make the equation balance (A = L&E), the residual claims (equity) must increase.

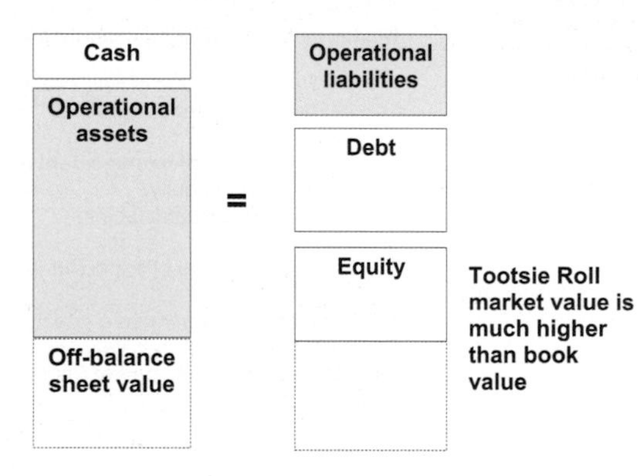

The **book** value for Tootsie Roll is $527m. The **market** value for Tootsie Roll is:

Outstanding class A shares	34,193	= 34,248 – 55
Outstanding class B shares	16,759	
Total outstanding shares	50,952	
x the current share price	$30.68	
= Market value of equity	$1,563m	

The market value added or goodwill (the difference between the book value and the market value of the shares, i.e. the market capitalization) is $1,036m.

SIMPLIFYING THE MARKET VALUE BALANCE SHEET

Most analysts simplify the market value balance sheet calculation, which you can do in two steps.

Step 1: Calculation of enterprise value

Net the operational liabilities against the operational assets and future growth opportunities. The net number is known as Enterprise Value, Firm Value, Asset Value or Aggregate Value.

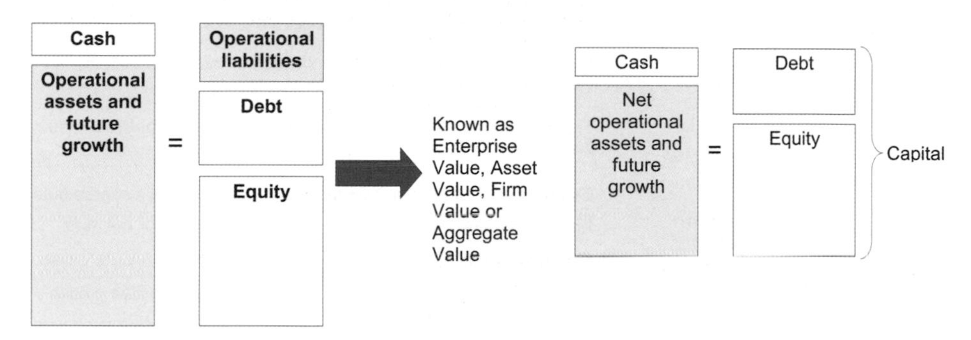

Step 2: Calculation of net debt
Net cash against debt to produce *net debt.*

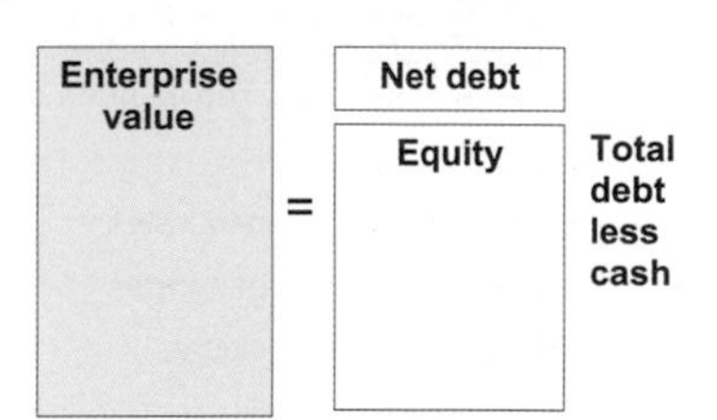

Tootsie Roll's Enterprise Value

- The market capitalization of Tootsie Roll in the previous example was $1,563,207.
- The total value of short and long-term debt on Tootsie Roll's balance sheet is $7,500.
- The value of cash on Tootsie Roll's balance sheet is $105,507.
- The value of short-term investments on Tootsie Roll's balance sheet is $40,737. We treat short-term investments as cash equivalents.

Calculating enterprise value:

Equity value	1,563,207
+ debt	7,500
- cash	105,507
- short-term investments	40,737
= Enterprise value	1,424,463

ENTERPRISE VALUE TO EQUITY VALUE – AND BACK

Enterprise value represents the market value of the company's net operational assets plus the value of its future growth opportunities and intangible assets not on the balance sheet.

Equity value represents the market value of the shareholders' investment in the business.

The following equations provide simple conversions between equity and enterprise value:

Slang!

Market cap is short for market capitalisation
EV is short for Enterprise Value

Equity value (market capitalization) =	Share price x shares outstanding
Enterprise value =	Market cap + net debt
Enterprise value =	Market cap + debt - cash
Equity value =	Enterprise value + cash – debt

ENTERPRISE AND EQUITY VALUE AND THE INCOME STATEMENT

Examine the previous equation in more detail (equity value = enterprise value + cash – debt). You can relate the calculation of equity value to the layout of the income statement. Later on we'll calculate ratios using our market value balance sheet and income statement numbers. The diagram below will be our "roadmap":

Balance sheet		**Income statement**
Enterprise value	generates	Operating profit
+ Cash	generates	+ Interest income
- Debt	claims	- Interest expense
		-Tax expense (unique to I/S)
= Equity value	claims	= Net income

Basic Comparables

COMPARABLE VALUATION

The most common means of valuing an asset is to find the prices of similar assets. For example, if you want to sell a house, you would look at the prices of comparable houses for sale in the relevant area. You would expect your house price to be similar to the prices of comparable houses.

Analysts value companies in exactly the same way. But there is an additional problem: finding companies exactly like the one you want to value is impossible. A key issue is size. How can you compare companies which are similar but are of different sizes?

THE VALUE OF MULTIPLES

Think of office space, often priced by the square foot. If you buy a 1,000 square-foot office building for $10 million, you are paying $10,000 per square foot. So the multiple per square foot is 10,000.

If you saw another building with 2,000 square feet, you could use the multiple to arrive at an approximate price of $20 million.

Analysts use multiples to price similar companies of different sizes in terms of key financial indicators such as sales, earnings before tax and net income. A multiple relates the company's value to a driver of its future profitability.

MOST MULTIPLES ARE BASED ON PROFITS

Most multiples use current or projected profits to relate value to future profitability. The question is: which profit? Your possibilities include net income, earnings before tax, operating profit, or even sales in some cases.

A company with a profit multiple of 10 would be valued at 10 times its profits.

WHICH PROFIT NUMBER TO USE IN YOUR MULTIPLE?

Always compare enterprise values using profits before interest. Always compare equity values using profits after interest.

As a shareholder (equity holder), you do not have a claim on the operating profit. You own what is remaining after paying interest expense and taxes.

Balance sheet		**Income statement**
Enterprise value	generates	Operating profit
+ Cash	*generates*	*+ Interest income*
- Debt	*claims*	*- Interest expense*
	-	*Tax expense (unique to I/S)*
= Equity value	claims	= Net income

Brett Bungee Jumping

You research the following information about Brett Bungee Jumping:

- Share price 12
- Shares outstanding 100
- Total debt 400
- Total cash and ST investments 100

Using the above information you calculate the valuation roadmap.
EBIT = Earnings Before Interest and Taxes = 150.

Balance sheet at market values		Income statement		Implied multiple
Enterprise value	1,500	EBIT	150	10 x EBIT multiple
+ cash	100	Interest income	3	
- debt	400	Interest expense	28	
		Tax expense	38	
= Equity value	1,200	Profit after tax	87	14 x Price earnings multiple

CALCULATING MULTIPLES

You face three issues when valuing a company using multiples:

1. Which universe(s) of companies to use as comparables
2. Which multiples to use
3. How to calculate the multiples accurately

IDENTIFYING/SELECTING COMPARABLES

Multiples valuation starts with identifying appropriate comparable companies. Take the perspective of an investor in equities (shares) when you are identifying comparables. Equity investors focus on companies' future profitability, so choose companies with comparable drivers of future profitability.

- A cellular phone company's future profits are driven by the number/mix of subscribers
- An electricity utility's future profits are driven by forecast general economic activity
- An auto-component manufacturing company's profits are driven by new car sales

Keep the number of comparables manageable - no more than 8 -10. Make sure that at least 50% of the comparable companies' business is in the same industry sector.

In general, to identify the appropriate combination of companies you should analyze the following factors:

- Business mix
- Margins
- Geographic spread of sales
- Recent and forecast investment, i.e. growth in property, plant and equipment (PP&E)
- Size (large companies are more resilient in a downturn and have more liquid stocks than smaller ones so investors generally put a premium on larger businesses)
- Growth rate of sales, profits and customers, if applicable
- Quality and number of clients
- Recent, current and forecast profitability

COMPARABLES CHECKLIST

The following ratios and key numbers will help you choose companies with similar future profitability drivers:

Metric	**What it tells you**
Market cap	Size of share capital, large companies' shares tend to be more liquid & therefore trade on a higher multiple
Sales	Size of business
Capital expenditure	Intensity of investment in the business as a driver for future profit growth
Industry mix	Different products can grow at different rates and/or have very different profitability
Geographical sales mix	Important, particularly if in different countries
Profit margins	The businesses' profitability
Expected EPS growth	Future growth in earnings – very important, a key driver of value
Unlevered beta	Volatility of earnings from assets

WHERE TO FIND COMPARABLES

- Use the standard industrial classification codes (SIC codes) in industry searches
- Research company databases, e.g. Bloomberg, Datastream, Reuters, etc.
- Ask an industry expert or someone who has recently completed a transaction in the industry
- Look at the company's competitors
- Review specialist industry publications
- Look at broker reports

WHICH MULTIPLE?

You can choose to use either an enterprise or an equity value multiple. Remember, enterprise multiples use earnings ***above*** the interest line; equity multiples use earnings ***below*** the interest line.

EQUITY MULTIPLES

Equity Multiples use earnings below the interest line

Equity multiples compare the value of common shares to the earnings available to common shareholders. Use equity multiples to calculate the value of a company's equity.

PRICE EARNINGS RATIO (PE RATIO OR PER)

The Price Earnings ratio is one of the most commonly used multiples. It can be calculated in two ways:

1. $$PE = \frac{\textbf{Market cap}}{\textbf{Net income to common shareholders}}$$

2. $$PE = \frac{\textbf{Share price}}{\textbf{Earnings per share}}$$

Tootsie Roll's PE ratio

Tootsie Roll's market capitalization (market value of equity) is $1,563,207. On Tootsie's income statement the company records net earnings of $66,388. Using the equity value and net earnings numbers you can calculate the PE ratio:

$$23.5x = \frac{1,563,207}{66,388}$$

Alternatively you can use the share price $30.68 and earnings per share number $1.29:

$$23.8x = \frac{30.68}{1.29}$$

Hold on, you get a slightly different answer! The earnings per share method uses the weighted average shares outstanding for the year. The net earnings number uses shares outstanding at one point in time. Which should you use?

Using the shares outstanding number at one point in time (the net earnings calculation) is more accurate as it is a better approximation of future price earnings ratios. Use the earnings per share method if you are short of time.

Some analysts like to use the earnings per share method to be consistent with market practice.

In spite of its popularity as a comparable, the PE ratio has some weaknesses:

- Different companies in the same sector may have different accounting policies/rules, which may distort earnings after tax
- One-off expenses or income may suppress or increase earnings, distorting your view of the company's long-term profitability
- A company's leverage (amount of debt) can affect earnings but is not a driver of its long-term profitability

If a company has a relatively high forecast long-term growth rate it should have a high price earnings ratio. Remember, the value of a company is reflected by its expected future earnings, not in its historical profits.

Real Estate companies & financial institutions

can revalue assets because they are in the business of trading those assets (houses, bond portfolios and other securities)

BOOK VALUE MULTIPLES

Some industries such as finance or real estate revalue their balance sheet assets every year. When the assets change in value and the liabilities remain constant, then the equity value will have to change too. A common multiple used in these industries is the multiple of market value to book value.

$$\text{Book value multiple} = \frac{\text{Market cap}}{\text{Book value}}$$

As with PE multiples, accounting differences and the impact of different levels of financial leverage can easily distort book value multiples. Unfortunately, there are no easy adjustments to correct this problem.

Tootsie Roll's book value multiple

Take Tootsie Roll's market capitalization of $1,563,207 and divide by the book value of Tootsie Roll's shareholders' equity on the balance sheet $526,740:

$$3.0x = \frac{1,563,207}{526,740}$$

Enterprise value multiples must use earnings before interest

ENTERPRISE VALUE MULTIPLES

Enterprise multiples compare the value of the enterprise to the profits generated by the firm. They are used to calculate the enterprise (or firm) value of the target company. They are popular because they make adjusting for non-recurring items easy and they are not affected by financial leverage (debt levels) because they use profits before interest payable on debt.

EBIT MULTIPLES

EBIT = Earnings Before Interest and Tax. EBIT multiples use earnings before both interest income and interest expense.

A multiple compares an asset's value to the profits generated by the asset. Be careful not to include income the asset does not generate. For example, Enterprise Value does ***not*** include the value of cash, so do not include interest income in your EBIT number.

$$\text{EBIT multiple} = \frac{\text{Enterprise value}}{\text{EBIT}}$$

A popular multiple for experts!

EBITDA MULTIPLES

EBITDA = Earnings Before Interest, Tax, Depreciation, and Amortization.

A company can choose how long it amortizes or depreciates an asset. This is driven by the accounting standards of the country, industry and, sometimes tax considerations. Consequently, companies with different depreciation policies calculate their earnings differently. How can you compare them? By removing depreciation and amortization from both companies' profits.

EBITDA removes the impact of differences between respective depreciation and amortization policies, leveling the playing field among different companies.

$$\textbf{EBITDA multiple} = \frac{\textbf{Enterprise value}}{\textbf{EBITDA}}$$

Itlay Inc

Remember the roadmap from a previous example:

Balance sheet at market values		**Income statement**		**Multiple**	
Enterprise value	1,500	EBIT	150	10 x	EBIT multiple
+ cash	100	Interest income	3		
- debt	400	Interest expense	28		
		Tax expense	38		
= Equity value	1,200	Profit after tax	87	14 x	Price earnings multiple

Using the information below you can calculate Itlay Inc.'s valuation roadmap:

Share price	15
Shares outstanding	200
Total debt	600
Cash	150
Depreciation expense	100
Amortization expense	40
EBIT	400
Interest income	6
Interest expense	20
Tax expense	116

Balance sheet at market values		Income statement		Multiple	
		EBITDA	540	6.4x	EBITDA multiple
		Depreciation	100		
		Amortization	40		
Enterprise value	3,450	EBIT	400	9 x	EBIT multiple
+ cash	150	Interest income	6		
- debt	600	Interest expense	20		
		Tax expense	116		
= Equity value	3,000	Profit after tax	270	11 x	Price earnings multiple

REVENUE OR SALES MULTIPLES

In some cases analysts go right to the top of the income statement and compare enterprise value to sales.

$$\text{Revenue multiple} = \frac{\text{Enterprise value}}{\text{Revenues}}$$

Be careful with revenue multiples because sales do not tell you anything about the company's profitability. Revenue multiples can be useful when analyzing a business which has yet to achieve positive earnings as the best approximation to future profitability.

REVENUE MULTIPLES AND UNPROFITABLE COMPANIES

Some companies maybe report losses rather than profits, although they might become profitable over the long-term. You cannot calculate a multiple for a loss making firm. So how do you value a firm which makes losses now but will turn to profit in the future?

If the company is reporting a net loss to shareholders do not use net income. Move up the income statement to EBIT. Profits still negative? Move up to EBITDA. *Still* negative? Move up to sales.

During the dot com boom of the late 1990s a number of companies being listed on the stock market were not reporting any profits. Most of them could be valued on revenues only.

USING MULTIPLES TO VALUE UNQUOTED COMPANIES

If a company is not quoted on a stock exchange how are you going to establish its value? Similar companies trade on similar multiples. You can use the comparable companies multiples to value the unquoted firm. Use the following steps:

1. Find a set of comparable companies to the firm you want to value.
2. Calculate a set of multiples for each comparable company.

Calculate the enterprise and equity value of the unquoted firm assuming it would trade on a similar multiple to your comparables.

Newcastle Deep Fried Mars Bars Ltd

You are advising a large food company who wants to acquire Newcastle Deep Fried Mars Bars Ltd. After careful research you establish two close comparables; Harrogate Chip Butties Ltd and Bristol Cornish Pasties Co. Ltd. You do not have a share price for Newcastle. You plan to use multiples.

Step 1

You prepare a small comparables sheet:

	Newcastle	**Harrogate**	**Bristol**
Sales	23,000	20,000	18,000
Depreciation	250	300	200
Amortization	30	30	30
Operating profit	**1,000**	**800**	**500**
Other income	20	10	30
EBIT	**1,020**	**810**	**530**
Interest expense	100	200	200
Earnings before tax	**920**	**610**	**330**
Tax expense @ 20%	(184)	(122)	(66)
Earnings after tax	736	488	264
Equity capitalization	???	3,936	2,904
Net	1,250	2,857	3,000
Enterprise value	???	6,793	5,904
Number of shares	1,000		
EBITDA multiple	N/A	???	???

Step 2

First calculate the EBITDA multiples of the two comparables. Then calculate the implied value of Newcastle:

	Harrogate	**Bristol**
EBIT	810	530
Depreciation	300	200
Amortization	30	30
EBITDA	1,140	760
Enterprise value	6,793	5,904

Calculate Harrogate's EBITDA multiple

EBITDA multiple 6.0x = 6,793 / 1,140

Calculate Bristol's EBITDA multiple

EBITDA multiple 7.8x = 5,904 / 760

Step 3

Use Harrogate's and Bristol's EBITDA multiple to calculate an implied Enterprise Value for Newcastle.

Newcastle's EBITDA 1,300 = 1,020 + 250 + 30

Calculate Newcastle's implied Enterprise Value

Using Harrogate's EBITDA multiple	7,800	= 6.0 x 1,300
Using Bristol's EBITDA multiple	10,140	= 7.8 x 1,300

Now calculate Newcastle's implied share price using the implied enterprise multiple.

Using Harrogate's multiple

Implied enterprise value	7,800
Less net	1,250
= Implied equity value	6,550
Divide by number of shares	1,000
= Implied share price	£6.55

Using Bristol's multiple

Implied enterprise value	10,140
Less net	1,250
= Implied equity value	8,890
Divide by number of shares	1,000
= Implied share price	£8.89

Newcastle should be valued at between £6.55 and £8.89 a share.

HOW TO CALCULATE MULTIPLES ACCURATELY

Do not just jump to the annual report and grab any headline earnings number. Companies are individuals; they're all slightly different. Each has its own quirks, which you must take into account.

Key differences which may need to be taken into account:

- Financial period, e.g. a number of companies have a 31st March year-end
- Interim announcements
- Non-recurring items
- Impact of a merger, acquisition or disposal during the financial reporting period
- Impact of a share issue, buyback or other financial engineering during the reporting period

When you are calculating multiples using projected (future) earnings, do not project Enterprise Value or Equity Value. They are calculated as of today.

CURRENT OR FUTURE EARNINGS?

Estimating the future profitability of a company is the driving force behind valuation. Analysts pay more attention to forecast earnings than to historical earnings. Use current period or future projected earnings, in addition to historical numbers, when you calculate multiples.

Justin's Bar Limited

You are preparing a multiple valuation of Justin's Bar Ltd. The following information is available for Justin:

Share price	23
Shares outstanding	300
Total net	1,200
Cash	300
Y+1 EBITDA (forecast)	500
Y+2 EBITDA (forecast)	550
Y+3 EBITDA (forecast)	610

Step 1: Calculate enterprise value

Equity value	6,900	= 23 * 300
+ total net	1,200	
- cash	300	
= Enterprise value	7,800	

Step 2: Calculate the forward looking multiples:

Year	Enterprise value	EBITDA	Multiple
Y+1	7,800	500	15.6 x
Y+2	7,800	550	14.2 x
Y+3	7,800	610	12.8 x

Notice the forward looking multiples get smaller the further out you go. If your forward looking multiples do not get smaller you have probably made a mistake. Check for the existence of a non-recurring item in the historical period. If you find a non-recurring item you need to normalize the historical earnings.

NORMALIZING EARNINGS

Many times you'll see one-off expenses or income on an income statement. "One-off" means they will not recur. If you include them in your calculation of the multiple, they will distort your multiples and therefore your valuation. Your earnings number in a multiple should reflect the company's underlying profitability, not a one-time event.

Common examples of one-off events include:

- Restructuring costs
- Fluctuating other income / expenses
- Extraordinary items "above the line"
- Large asset impairments
- Large gain/loss on disposals
- Accounting changes

When you are using earnings before interest and taxes (EBIT or EBITDA) to calculate a multiple, just add back the non-recurring expenses and subtract the non-recurring income.

When you are using earnings after tax, things get a little more complicated. A change in earnings also affects taxes, you must also alter the tax expense:

	Actual (before adjustment)	Adjustment	Normalized (after adjustment)
Restructuring costs	50		0
Profit before tax	100	+50	150
Tax	30	+15 = 50*30%	45
Net income	70	+35	105

Explanation

Profit before tax goes up by	50	
So tax has to go up too		
Tax rate is	30%	
Tax increases by	15	(50 * 30%)
Net income rises by a net	35	(50 -15)

Analyst's shortcut!

Go directly to the new profit number in one step:

Multiply the increase in profit by (1 – tax rate)

50 * (1 – 30%) = 35

70 + 35 = 105

Always use the ***marginal tax rate*** (the tax rate on incremental income) when you are adjusting for non-recurring items.

LAST TWELVE MONTHS (LTM)

In the US, companies file quarterly financial reports (10Q) as well as year-end reports (10K), typically one to two months after the end of the reporting period. If investors relied only on year-end financial statements, their earnings number could be out-of-date by up to 12 months or more.

You can create a more up-to-date profit number by combining the information found in quarterly and annual reports. Of course this process applies only to US companies, as most other countries do not require quarterly reporting. UK listed companies usually file interims six months after the company's year-end.

About the 10Q

The 10Q will report at least three different sets of earnings:

- Current quarter
- Year-to-date for this financial year (if more than one quarter since the last financial year-end)
- Previous financial year's year-to-date and quarter

The LTM process

Converting information to LTM is the same for all income statement multiples.

As an illustration, assume that you are calculating an EBIT multiple for a company whose last-year end was December 31, Year n. They have just reported the first quarter's 10Q (the three months to March 31 Year n+1). Here's what you do:

Step 1. Start with the earnings number from the annual report.

EBIT from the annual report is 1,000.

Step 2. Add the latest earnings number found in the 10Q.

Find this year's year-to-date EBIT number for the 10Q. In our example you'd look for the YTD number from January 1, Year n+1 to March 31, Year n+1. Assume that number is 400.

Adjusted EBIT so far: 1,400 (=1,000 + 400).

Step 3. Subtract the last year's year-to-date earnings number found in the 10Q.

Find the EBIT from the oldest quarter to March 31 Year n. Assume that number is 300.

LTM EBIT: 1,100 (=1,000 + 400 – 300)

James Surfing Co.

James Surfing Co. has a year end of 31 December. James recently reported third quarter earnings for 2006. You want to calculate James' multiples as at November 1st 2006. You prepare a table of multiples information to calculate the last twelve month numbers (LTM):

	2005 10K	9mths to Sept 05	9mths to Sept 06	LTM
Revenue	1,000	700	800	1,100
EBITDA	400	80	120	440
EBIT	200	40	60	220

The last twelve months number is calculated by taking the full year number for 2005, subtracting the nine months to September 05 (the old earnings) and adding the nine months to September 06 (the new earnings).

Next calculate the enterprise value at the date of valuation:

Share price at November 1st	34
Shares outstanding (from Sept 06 10Q)	50
Total debt (from Sept 06 10Q)	800
Cash (from Sept 06 10Q)	200
Enterprise value	2,300

LTM multiples

Revenue	2.1 x	= 2,300 / 1,100
EBITDA	5.2 x	= 2,300 / 440
EBIT	10.5 x	= 2,300 / 220

LTM is sometimes also called TTM ("Trailing Twelve Months").

ANNUALIZATION OR CALENDARIZATION

Annualization is similar to the Last Twelve Months adjustment. It requires you to adjust the earnings numbers because of timing issues.

The companies in your set of comparables may not have consistent year-end dates. You can adjust for these timing differences by ***annualizing*** the data.

Annualization or calendarization means you must calculate a time-weighted average of two year-end numbers. You're taking part of one year and adding it to part of another year to adjust for different year- ends. Now all your comparable companies will have consistent time periods.

Shoreditch, WasteStepney & Rubbish

You are calculating EBIT for comparable companies in the waste management sector. One of your companies has a different year-end. You must convert that company's numbers so that all your companies have the same year-end and you are comparing apples to apples.

	Shoreditch 31st Mar	WasteStepney 31st Dec	Rubbish 31st Dec
2005 EBIT	80		
2006 EBIT	90	98	60
2007 EBIT (projected)	100	108	80
2008 EBIT (projected)	110	118	100
2009 EBIT (projected)	120		

Take Shoreditch's EBIT numbers and convert them to a December 31 year-end. Shoreditch's actual year end is 31st March. It's "behind" WasteStepney and Rubbish's. One quarter = 25% or 3/12 of the year. Take 25% of Shoreditch's current year and 75% of Shoreditch's next year to create a rolling average.

Shoreditch annualized:

		31st Dec
2006 EBIT	90*25% + 100*75%	= 97.5
2007 EBIT	100*25% + 110*75%	= 107.5
2008 EBIT	110*25% + 120*75%	= 117.5

You can now compare Shoreditch's numbers to WasteStephney and Rubbish.

Advanced Comparable Valuation

Before you continue, you should have a firm understanding of how to calculate simple multiples accurately.

Now for the hard parts. Two areas will create difficulty for you when you calculate multiples:

1. Adjustments for different accounting standards between your comparables
2. Unusual or tricky financing items in the financial statements.

DIFFERENT ACCOUNTING POLICIES

Comparable companies may account for the same item in different ways, distorting the data. You might want to adjust for the following items, especially if they make a big difference to your final numbers.

INVESTMENTS

Investments fall into two classifications: strategic and financial. Remember that you must match the asset with the income it generates. Strategic investments are a component of enterprise value. The income from strategic investments should be included in the earnings number you compare to enterprise value.

Financial investments should not be accounted for in enterprise value, so the income they generate should not be included in the earnings number you compare to enterprise value.

What is the difference between strategic and financial?

Establishing the difference between strategic and financial investments is not easy. As a rule of thumb, long-term investments are generally strategic (unless they are not related to the core business of the parent company). Short-term investments are more likely to be financial in nature.

Sometimes the rule of thumb does not work

Long-term assets which do not help the core operation of the business should be treated as financial investments. For example, in the late 1970s some film studios were losing money but were still valuable because of their land holdings in southern California.

The studios had bought the land decades before and occasionally used it for cowboy movies. In the 1970s, the impact of inflation combined with the growth of housing and businesses in southern California, these land holdings became valuable.

Owning that land was not critical to the film studios' core business. Analysts treated the land as a financial investment and excluded it from enterprise value. Although valuable, the land generated very little immediate income and would distort comparisons to studios which owned no land.

Remember, when you exclude an asset from EV, you must also exclude from your earnings number the income that asset generates.

EQUITY METHOD INVESTMENTS: CONTROL OR CONSOLIDATED?

When a company owns between 20% and 50% of another business, it accounts for the stake in the other company as an equity method investment (in some accounting jurisdictions equity method investments are defined as where the shareholder has "significant influence").

Each year, the company will show on its income statement its share of the other business's profit. The account is called equity income (or associate or affiliate income). The company also adds the equity income to the equity investment shown on its balance sheet.

Should you treat an investment like this as a strategic investment? In most cases, the answer is yes.

Control freaks!

In the 1990s, Vodafone (the UK mobile phone company) acquired Mannesmann (a German mobile phone company). When Vodafone was valuing Mannesman it put a higher multiple on the earnings which Mannesmann controlled. Mannesmann also had equity income which it, of course, did not control. Analysts placed a lower multiple on the equity income. Control was important to Vodafone as it could use the cash flow from controlled operations to invest in new cellular technology (third generation or 3G) for other operations.

The Vodafone case is pretty unusual. In most cases you want to treat equity method investments as part of the enterprise value.

Valuing equity method investments

If you do want to exclude the value of equity method investments from enterprise value, as in the Vodafone/Mannesman case, you still need to value the investment.

You already know the market value of most companies' equity is higher than the value of their book equity. The balance sheet value of equity method investments is the original cost plus the company's share of any retained profits. Similarly, the market value of the investment could be very different.

If the other company is quoted on an exchange, it is easy to get the investment's market value. If not, you can use a PE multiple to multiply the share of earnings on the income statement and secure a reasonable estimate of the investment's market value.

Some countries present equity income as a share of operating profit. You can convert the share of operating profit to a share of net income by finding the investment's share of tax and interest in the notes. Subtract the relevant tax and interest items to get to net income.

Strategic versus financial investments

You want to compare the value of two quoted mobile telecom companies. They both have a significant affiliate (equity method investments). You know the market values controlled cash flows more highly than associate dividends.

	Germany	UK	
Company	**Mobile T**	**Purple**	
Operating profit	120.0	60.0	
EBIT	120.0	60.0	
Depreciation and amortization	40.0	20.0	
Affiliate income	10.0	5.5	
Shares outstanding	234.0	500.0	
Share price	6.0	1.5	
Equity value	1,404.0	750.0	= 1.5 * 500
Net debt excluding associate	456.0	400.0	
Other information			
PE multiple for assoc value	12.0	12.0	
Assoc share of PAT	10.0	5.5	
Implied associate value	120.0	66.0	= 5.5 * 12
Net debt inc. assoc as cash	336.0	334.0	= 400 – 66
Controlled Enterprise value	1,740.0	1,084.0	= 750 + 334
Controlled EBITDA	160.0	80.0	= 60 + 20
Controlled EBITDA multiple	10.9 x	13.6 x	= 1,084 / 80

The controlled EBITDA multiple is valuing only the controlled earnings of the business.

Employee stock options

When you converted enterprise value to equity value, you added cash and subtracted debt, assuming that no other claims on earnings existed. A common claim on earnings that we have not discussed yet is the employee stock option.

Stock options give their holders the right to buy stock at a fixed price. If the current share price is above the option's fixed price, the stock options can be quite valuable, but these do not appear on the balance sheet until the options are actually exercised. You must value this hidden residual claim.

You can use one of two methods, the intrinsic method and the treasury method:

Note to Experts

The treasury method is also used in the diluted earnings per share calculation with the exception that the diluted earnings per share uses an average share price, not the current share price.

Intrinsic method

$$\text{Market value of options} = [\text{share price} - \text{exercise price}] * \text{number of options}$$

Treasury method

$$\text{Market value of options} = \frac{[\text{share price} - \text{exercise price}]}{\text{share price}} * \text{number of options} * \text{share price}$$

Short Telecommunications Inc

You want to calculate the EBITDA multiple for Short Telecommunications. You know the company has a great deal of executive share options outstanding. By issuing the options the company has given away future upside to the executives. We need to reflect the value of the options in our analysis.

	Employees	Executives	
Options	1,200.0	3,000.0	
Strike price	10.0	12.0	
Share price	15.0	15.0	
Intrinsic value	6,000.0	9,000.0	= (15 - 12) * 3,000
Treasury method			
Cash from issued options	12,000.0	36,000.0	= 12 * 3,000
Shares repurchased	800.0	2,400.0	= 36,000 / 15
Net new shares issued	400.0	600.0	= 3,000 - 2,400
Value of options	6,000.0	9,000.0	= 600 * 15

PREFERRED STOCK

Legally, preferred stock is an equity account. Its claim on assets is subordinate to all liabilities. However, unlike common equity, its claim is fixed, not residual. It has a fixed claim against the assets of the business and pays a fixed dividend. Preference share dividends must be paid before common equity holders receive anything.

Because preference shares have a fixed claim against the assets of the business, their market value is usually close to book value. Many analysts treat preference shares like debt for valuation purposes. Beware that there are many different preference share structures.

Valuing preferred stock

If the preferred shares are quoted on the Stock Exchange, use the market value of the preferred stock in your valuation. Many analysts use the book value as an acceptable short cut.

UNDER OR OVERFUNDED PENSION ASSETS AND LIABILITIES

Many companies allow employees to contribute to in-house pension plans. In a defined benefit plan, the company guarantees the amount of payout at retirement. But perhaps the company will not have invested enough financial assets to meet the pension obligations in the future. If the pension assets are lower than the pension obligation, the plan is "underfunded." If the pension assets are higher than the pension obligation, the plan is "overfunded."

In continental Europe and Japan defined benefit pensions are generally unfunded, i.e. companies will show a provision for future pension liabilities.

Pension accounting is notoriously complicated. The two main complications:

1. If the pension plan is either under or overfunded, the difference does not immediately appear on the balance sheet.

2. You might suspect that accounting treats the unfunded and underfunded pension as a financing liability, but accounting principles consider it to be an operational liability.

Pensions and valuation

When you are valuing you should stick to your original thought and treat unfunded and underfunded pensions as a financing liability. But what do you do about the accounting? You make an adjustment.

Go to the pension note in the annual report. Find the fair value of the pension plan assets and the pension obligation. If the fair value is higher than the obligation, the plan is overfunded. If it is lower than the obligation, the plan is underfunded.

Essential information about pensions

1. If the pension is not over or underfunded, it will not appear on the financial statements at all.
2. The pension fund is a separate entity.
3. The company's contributions to the pension fund are tax-deductible.
4. Repayments to the company from the pension fund might occur if the fund is overfunded. These repayments are taxable.
5. For valuation purposes, if the pension is underfunded, assume that the company has to take out a loan to meet the shortfall. If the pension is overfunded, assume the company extracts the surplus as cash.

How to adjust for over or underfunded pensions

Only adjust for the over or underfunded pension amount. Remember the relationships between the market value balance sheet and income statement:

Balance sheet		**Income statement**
Enterprise value	generates	Operating profit
+ Cash	generates	+ Interest income
- Debt	claims	- Interest expense
		-Tax expense (unique to I/S)
= Equity value	claims	= Net income

Pensions are treated as an operational activity on the financial statements. If the accounting model treats pensions as an operational activity, then the under or overfunded pension will be included in enterprise value (like all other operational liabilities). Any costs or income associated with the pension will be included in operating profit.

You must adjust enterprise value and operating profit by removing the interest expense or income related to the under or overfunded portion of the pension. Remember, contributions to the pension fund are tax-deductible and repayments are taxable. So your adjustment has a tax impact.

OVER FUNDED PENSION ADJUSTMENT

An example will help make the adjustment clear.

Cleo

Cleo Inc.'s pension plan is overfunded by 100m.

Balance sheet adjustment

If you are valuing Cleo, you should assume any surplus will be taken from the pension plan as cash. The cash will be treated as income and will be taxed like any other income. The net gain to Cleo is not 100m but 100m minus the tax.

Assume the tax rate is 30%.

100m * (1 – 30%) = 70m

Cleo's cash increases by 70m, not 100m.

Income statement adjustment

Here is a sequence of consequences:

1. The benefit of surplus cash in any pension reduces the pension expense on the income statement.
2. If you treat the pension surplus as cash then you no longer want the reduction of pension expense on the income statement.
3. You only want to include the ongoing service cost in your pension expenses.
4. Taking out the benefit of the pension surplus will reduce the company's operating profit.

I have shown you the correct method for calculating the net over or underfunded pension. However, some research on these issues shows that the market does not adjust the under or overfunded pension asset or liability for tax impact. Under or overfunded pensions have only become a significant issue recently. Perhaps investors aren't aware of these issues yet!

Applied to Cleo

In Cleo's accounts you see the following information about the company's pension expense:

Service cost	(100)
Interest cost	(20)
Expected return on plan assets	30
Amortization of prior service cost	10
Amortization of net gains	(10)
Pension expense	(90)

The most important number in the table above is the service cost. The service cost represents the current year's cost of pension expenses. All the other costs relate to pension costs accrued from prior years.

Adjust Cleo's operating profit as though the only pension expense was the service cost:

Operating profit	500
+ Unadjusted pension expense	90
- Service cost	(100)
Adjusted operating profit	490

For more detail on the accounting behind pensions check our Advanced Accounting Midnight Manual

The consequences for valuation of overfunded pension funds

You must make two adjustments for overfunded pension schemes:

1. Calculate the surplus cash after tax. Include this number in your enterprise value calculations.
2. Adjust your before-interest earnings number (EBIT, EBITDA) so you only include the pension service cost for the current year.

The consequences for valuation of underfunded pension funds

You must make two adjustments for underfunded pension schemes:

1. Calculate the equivalent debt liability after tax. Remember we assume that the company takes out a loan to meet the pension fund deficit. Include this number in your enterprise value calculations.
2. Adjust your before-interest earnings number (EBIT, EBITDA) so you only include the pension service cost for the current year.

Germany: an exceptional case

In some countries, such as Germany, there is no legal requirement to make payments into a separate pension fund. The company itself usually acts as the pension fund. German pension liabilities appear on the balance sheet and may be hidden in an account called Provisions. Some of the pension costs may also be in the interest expense line item.

OTHER POST-EMPLOYMENT BENEFITS

If you understand pensions, you'll understand other post-employment benefits. Some companies offer medical coverage to retired employees. Medical coverage does not show up in pension funds but has its own account, Other Post-Employment Benefits, sometimes nicknamed OPEBs. Sometimes it is buried in other long-term liabilities.

Companies do not set up a fund to cover OPEBs, so they are nearly always underfunded. Treat them the same way you would treat unfunded pension liabilities.

FINANCE AND OPERATING LEASES

When a company leases equipment, it is providing itself with long-term financing for the asset. It can account for its leases in two different ways:

- As an operating lease. Accounting treats operating leases like rentals. The accounts show only an expense on the income statement and no asset or liabilities on the Balance Sheet.
- As a capitalized lease (also known as finance lease). Accounting treats capitalized leases as though the company used a loan to purchase the leased asset. The company records the depreciation of the asset and the interest expense from the loan on the income statement. The balance of the loan and the undepreciated amount of the asset appear on the balance sheet.

Why is this important to valuation? A company with operating leases expenses them before interest; they are part of EBITDA. A company with finance leases expenses the lease in the depreciation and interest lines, which are not included in EBITDA.

Companies may have operating and finance leases at the same time.

Any time you are comparing companies and they have different accounting policies, you have a problem. You need to make the accounting for leases consistent across all companies.

To convert between operating and finance leases

Most analysts convert operating to finance leases, not the other way around. You can only make the conversion for EBITDA and revenue multiples. You want to see income before the cost of the financing; finance leases affect depreciation expense, so you cannot use earnings after deducting depreciation expense (EBIT or net income).

A quick and dirty way of converting an operating lease to a finance lease is to use the rule of eight. Multiply the lease payment by eight. Eight times the lease payment is a rough equivalent for the finance lease liability.

When you convert an operating lease to a financing lease, you must adjust both EBITDA and enterprise value. Include the equivalent finance lease liability as debt in your calculation of enterprise value, just as you would for a finance lease.

All finance expenses are deducted after EBITDA. To convert to a finance lease, add back the operating lease expense to EBITDA.

Converting an operating lease to a financing lease

	Before	After
Lease expense	(10)	0
EBITDA	100	110
Lease liability	0	80
Enterprise value	1,000	1,080

The adjusted EBITDA number is known as EBITDAR (where R stands for operating lease rents). EBITDAR multiples are used in industries where large amounts of fixed assets are leased e.g. airlines.

Rule of eight, seven, nine?

The rule of eight is a common method of estimating the equivalent finance lease liability. In some industries people may use different multiples. Check what multiple is used for your target industry. It may be more or less than eight.

Alternative method

Alternatively, take the future planned operating lease payments from the notes in the annual report and discount them back to today (the finance lease equivalent liability). Use the company's cost of debt as your discount rate.

Interest rate	7.0%					
	Y0	Y1	Y2	Y3	Y4	Y5
Lease payments		90.0	80.0	56.0	45.0	30.0
Discount factor		93.5%	87.3%	81.6%	76.3%	71.3%
Present value		84.1	69.9	45.7	34.3	21.4
Debt equivalent	255.4					

CONVERTIBLE BONDS

Convertible bonds can convert from debt to shares (equity). They fall between the categories of debt and equity.

The value of convertible bonds includes the bond value plus the value of an option to convert the bonds into equity. It is likely that the market value of convertible bonds will be higher than their balance sheet value because of this option.

Your best strategy

Your best strategy is to look for the market value of the bonds. You can find their traded value by consulting Bloomberg. If you cannot find a traded price for the bonds, you must establish what their value would be if they convert into shares today.

First, find out how many shares the convertible bonds convert into. Look in the annual report for this information. Then calculate the market value of those shares. Take the higher number: the market value of the shares, or the balance sheet value of the bonds.

Share price	50.0	
Bonds amount (m)	100.0	
Bonds par value	1,000.0	
Number of bonds	100,000.0	= 100 / 1,000 * 1,000,000
Conversion ratio	25.0	
Market value of each bond	1,250.0	= 25 * 50
In the money by	250.0	= 1,250 - 1,000
Addition to number of shares (m)	2.5	=100,000 * 25 / 1,000,000
Addition to market capitalization (m)	125.0	125.0

If the number of shares is increased as in the above example, do not add the value of the convertible to net debt.

MEZZANINE FINANCING

Mezzanine finance has two parts: a loan and an option to buy equity. Unlike convertible bonds, the loan does not convert into equity. A mezzanine finance holder can buy shares at a fixed price as well as receive repayment for the loan.

Each part of mezzanine finance has value, the loan and the option. Find the value of the loan by looking on the balance sheet or in the notes. Easy!

What about the value of the common stock option? Use the same methods described under *Stock options*.

After you collect the value of the loan and the value of the option, add them together to get the value of the mezzanine finance.

Mezzanine loan	100.0	
Warrants on equity	10.0	
Share price	25.0	
Strike price	18.0	
Cash from warrants	180.0	= 10 * 18
Shares repurchased	7.2	= 180 / 25
Net new shares	2.8	= 10 - 7.2
Value of options	70.0	= 2.8 * 25
Value of loan	100.0	
Value of options	70.0	
Total value	170.0	= 100 + 70

MINORITY INTERESTS

A minority interest occurs when one company purchases a controlling stake in another but does not acquire 100% of the equity. Minority interest is the flip side of equity investment. In this case the company you are valuing is partially owned by another entity.

What is the difference between minority interest and a regular shareholder who owns some stock? A regular shareholder owns shares in the parent company. A minority interest holder owns shares in a subsidiary of the parent company.

MegaCorp has two subsidiaries, Twee and Bonnie Dunes. If Leslie buys shares in MegaCorp, she is a regular shareholder; she has bought shares in the parent company. But if she buys Bonnie Dunes shares, she is a minority interest holder; she has bought the subsidiary's shares, not the parent's.

MINORITY INTEREST ON THE FINANCIAL STATEMENTS

Minority interest appears on the financial statements in two places:

1. The consolidated income statement: the minority interest's share of the subsidiary's profit. Look for this figure just before net income.
2. The balance sheet: the minority interest's share of the subsidiary's book value appears in one of three places: the liabilities, the equity, or between liabilities and equity.

Book value is not usually a good measure of market value. The balance sheet value (book value) of the minority interest is likely to be lower than its market value.

VALUING MINORITY INTEREST

If the minority interest is quoted as a separate entity on a Stock Exchange, use the quoted value of the investment. If it is not quoted, take the share of the subsidiary's net income and multiply it by a relevant PE multiple (a multiple that is comparable to the subsidiary). If non-recurring items appear in the net income of the subsidiary, clean them out before you value.

Minority interest share of income	45	
Relevant PE multiple	11	
Implied value of minority interest	495	= 45 * 11

CATS AND DOGS

Below are some additional twists you need to bear in mind.

YIELD DRIVEN STOCKS

Shares with high dividend payout ratios typically have much lower PE ratios, reflecting less internal investment and ultimately slower growth. Check your comparables for differences in dividend payout rates and choose companies that are similar.

TRANSACTION MULTIPLES

THE CONCEPT OF CONTROL

People pay a premium to get control of a business. If they buy more than 50% of the company's equity, they have to pay extra – a premium – to acquire that controlling interest.

UNDERSTANDING THE CONTROL PREMIUM

Reasons why an acquirer will be willing to pay more for a company than its current share price:

1. The acquirer may want to prevent a competitor from purchasing the target.
2. The deal is a once-in-a-life-time opportunity or strategically significant.
3. The company is trading at a discount to its discounted cash flow value. This could be due to diversified holdings or being in an unattractive industry.
4. The acquirer's cost of capital is lower than the target's.
5. The acquirer's perception of the industry's future differs from the market's.
6. The acquirer is interested in the potential value from synergies after the transaction.

BASIC DEFINITION OF TRANSACTION MULTIPLES

Transaction multiples measure the control premium. Transaction multiples show how much more people will pay, over and above the stock price, to gain control of a business. They are derived from prices paid in previous acquisitions.

PROBLEMS SURROUNDING TRANSACTION MULTIPLES

- The industry may not have had many transactions. You may not get an accurate picture from the skimpy data available.

- Information may be incomplete or not disclosed. Companies are notorious for not disclosing full information about a transaction.
- Information quickly becomes dated as market conditions change. A valuation should be based on up-to-date transactions.
- Financing sources change. The availability of funding may have dried up or increased since prior transactions.

IMPORTANCE OF COMPARABLE TRANSACTIONS

- Clients want to know the industry's deal history, especially regarding the premiums paid in the past.
- When an industry is experiencing lots of M&A activity, transaction multiples become more important.
- Gives insights into:

  ✓ Control premiums
  ✓ Previous bidding strategies
  ✓ List of potential buyers in an industry

WHY PEOPLE WILL PAY A CONTROL PREMIUM

- Their views of a company's future differ from the market's.
- The combined company may have a lower cost of capital than either company separately.
- Synergies available to buyers (see below).
- Strategic reasons:

  ✓ If a company expands from within, it adds supply to the market, which puts pressure on prices to fall. By buying another company, a company can grow and avoid downward pressure on prices.
  ✓ A company can avoid being taken over by making an acquisition itself.

SYNERGIES

When you acquire control of a company, ***you*** decide the strategic direction it takes, so you can create value from synergies:

- Financial synergies - e.g. access to cheaper funding (immediate).
- Marketing synergies (2 to 3 years to generate). By taking one company's products and pushing them through another company's distribution network, you can expand market share with relatively little effort.
- Production synergies (5 to 10 years to generate). A bigger company should be able to generate larger economies of scale.
- Cost synergies (1 to 3 years to generate). The combined companies will need only one corporate headquarters building, one administrative function, one finance function and one marketing department.

Transaction	Pre-deal share price	Post-deal share price	Premium	EPS	Acquisition PE
Telecom Inc	15	23	53.3%	1.3	17.7
Teleco Ltd	23	30	30.4%	1.5	20.0
Phonco Pty	56	70	25.0%	3.0	23.3

DCF Valuation

OVERVIEW

The Discounted Cash Flow (DCF) approach to valuation is the most technically rigorous of all valuation methods. It values a business by taking its forecast future cash flows and discounting them back to today. Discounted Cash Flow has several advantages over multiples valuation:

- It's more likely to be accurate. DCF valuation rests on cash flows, not profits. Accounting policies can be used to manipulate profits, but not cash flows.
- It allows you to value the benefits of potential synergies in a transaction.
- It allows you to build a range of scenarios showing the impact on value based on different views of the company's future.

WHAT ARE THE DOWNSIDES OF USING A DCF VALUATION?

- It reflects only a single view of the business. You project the cash flows; you make the driving assumptions. The market may not agree with you on any of these points.
- The value is highly sensitive to the discount rate, particularly if you use the Gordon Growth Model to calculate the terminal value.

WHAT VALUE DO YOU GET FROM A DCF VALUATION?

DCF valuation focuses on the cash flows generated by one part of the business: the net operational assets. These cash flows are called ***free cash flows***. To create a DCF valuation, you forecast the free cash flows into the future, usually for a period of between five and ten years. You then discount them back to today to get an enterprise value.

NET OPERATIONAL ASSETS

The shaded areas in the diagram on the next page show you what net operational assets are: operational assets less operational liabilities. Operational assets include fixed assets or Net PP&E.

Another way of looking at net operational assets is to think of it as any asset or liability the company needs to help it create operating profit.

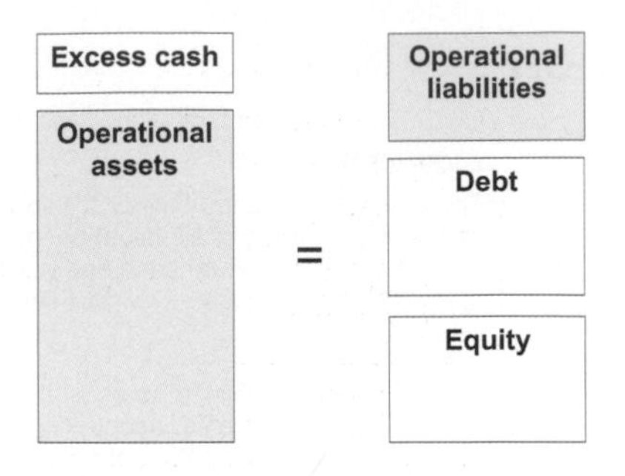

ABOUT FREE CASH FLOWS

A business generates cash through its daily operations of supplying and selling goods and/or services. Some of the cash has to go back into the business to renew fixed assets and support working capital. If the business is doing well, it should generate cash over and above these requirements. Any extra cash is free to go to the debt and equity holders. The extra cash is the free cash flow.

HOW TO CALCULATE FREE CASH FLOWS IN A NUTSHELL

Operating profit (EBIT)	Profit generated by net operational assets.
- Tax on operating profit (EBIT)	***Not*** tax expense on the income statement; it is affected by interest. Calculate the tax anew: Tax rate times operating profit.
+ Depreciation and tax - deductible amortization	This step converts operating profit into cash flow by adding back the non-cash expenses.
+ / - Change in operating working capital	This number captures the investment in operating working capital required to support the company's future activity.
- Capital expenditure	The new investment in fixed assets needed to support the company's future activity.
+ / - Change in other operational assets and liabilities	The "other stuff." May include long-term assets or liabilities needed to support the company's future activity.
= Free cash flows	Cash flows generated by the business after required investment. Available to pay out to both debt and equity holders.

Example – Ossining Tacos Ltd

Ossining Tacos forecast their free cash flow for the next three years:

	Y1	Y2	Y3
EBIT	100.0	120.0	150.0
Tax at 20%	20.0	24.0	30.0
EBIT after tax	80.0	96.0	120.0
+ depreciation	40.0	50.0	60.0
- capex	(40.0)	(50.0)	(50.0)
Change in OWC*	(15.0)	(16.0)	(18.0)
Free cash flow	65.0	80.0	112.0

**Excluding accounts driven by financing and investing activities*

A DETAILED LOOK AT FREE CASH FLOWS

Free cash flow is the cash you can distribute to both equity and debt holders while maintaining the business as a going concern.

OVERVIEW

Start with the after-tax operating profits from the business, add back any non-cash expenses, then subtract any investment required to sustain those profits.

AFTER-TAX PROFITS

1. Start by calculating earnings available to both the equity and debt holders, or EBIT.

   Do not make the mistake of taking earnings after interest. You need cash flows before any payments to both debt and equity holders.

2. Multiply EBIT by (1 less tax rate) to get EBIT after tax.

   Do not worry about the tax shield on interest; we will get to that later.

   You might see EBIT after tax called EBIAT (Earnings Before Interest After Tax) or NOPLAT (Net Operating Profit Less Adjusted Taxes).

NON-CASH CHARGES AND OTHER ADJUSTMENTS

3. Adjust for non-cash charges such as depreciation and amortization.

   Add back only tax-deductible amortization. If the company has non-tax-deductible amortization, add it to operating profit before you tax it.

INVESTMENT REQUIRED TO SUPPORT FUTURE CASH GENERATION

4. Subtract the investment required to support the cash flow generation in future.

   The two most common investment items are capital expenditure and operating working capital. Remember not to include non-operating current assets and liabilities, e.g. dividends payable, in operating working capital.

   Again, you might find other investing items you want to include, like other assets.

5. Do not include any financial investments in your investing activities. We will discuss financial investments later.

   Should you include equity method investments (associates/affiliates) in your free cash flows? No!

   Equity (associate) income is not cash income. Leave all your financial investments out of your free cash flows. Add financial investments on to your final present value number.

6. How long should you forecast? Most bankers forecast the free cash flows forward between five and ten years until the company reaches a ***steady state***. When a company has reached its steady state its growth is stable and predictable.

CALCULATE TERMINAL VALUE

In most valuation situations, analysts do not forecast a company's free cash flow out more than ten years. After ten years you cannot predict a company's free cash flows with any degree of certainty. Forecasts are usually between five and ten years long.

At the end of the forecast you assume the company reaches a "steady state". The best way of establishing whether a company has reached a steady state is to look at the ratios:

- Net fixed assets and operating working capital will remain a steady percentage of sales over time.
- The return on newly invested capital will be equal to or slightly higher than the company's weighted average cost of capital.

$$\textbf{RONIC} = \frac{\textbf{Change in EBIAT}}{\textbf{Change in invested capital}}$$

where	EBIAT =	EBIT less un-leveraged taxes
	Invested capital =	OWC + Net fixed assets + other operating assets – other operating liabilities

The company still has value after the forecast period. The value which the company creates after the forecast period is called the ***terminal*** value. You must capture that ongoing value in your valuation.

You can use one of three ways to estimate terminal value:

Terminal Value Multiple

Use a multiple to value the ongoing business after the forecast period. Estimate the value of the enterprise by multiplying either EBIT or EBITDA in the last year of the forecast by a suitable multiple.

Your multiple should reflect the ongoing growth potential of the business. At the end of your forecast the company's growth rate will probably be lower than at the beginning of your forecast, so your terminal multiple is likely to be lower than the multiple you would use to value the whole business today. Discount the terminal value to the beginning of your forecast.

Banbury Bakeries Ltd

Using an EBIT multiple of 11x, the terminal value for Banbury Bakeries is:

11 x 150 = 1,650

Assume the 1,650 is received **at the end** of year 2005 so discount it back three years. *Do not* make mid year adjustment for the terminal value.

	Y0	Y1	Y2	Y3
EBIT		100.0	120.0	150.0
Tax at 20%		20.0	24.0	30.0
Free cash flow		65.0	80.0	112.0
Terminal value				1,650.0

Gordon Growth Model

You can use financial maths. The growing perpetuity formula calculates the present value of a cash flow growing into infinity. Below is the shorthand for the formula:

$$\textbf{Terminal value} = \frac{\textbf{FCF}_n * (1 + g)}{(\textbf{WACC} - g)}$$

The full statement of the formula is below. Explanations follow:

$$\textbf{Terminal value} = \frac{\textbf{forecast free cashflow last projected year * (1 + LT growth rate)}}{\textbf{(discount rate - LT growth rate)}}$$

FCF Free cash flow, last projected year. You assume this number will grow into the future.

g Long-term growth rate of the cash flows. Usually g is above inflation but below nominal GDP growth. Companies cannot grow faster than the whole economy into perpetuity. You are assuming the company has reached a stable state (steady state) in the terminal period. Its terminal growth rate will usually be lower than the growth rate trend in the projected years.

WACC Weighted Average Cost of Capital, or the discount rate. You will learn about WACC in detail later.

WHY (1 + G)?

Mathematically, (1 + g) grows the last projected year out another year (to the first year of the perpetuity period). Why does the formula move the cash flows out another year?

The simple formula is: FCF / (WACC – g). This formula says: "Give me a constantly growing stream of cash flows that starts at the end of the year and I will show you the value of that cash flow stream at the beginning of the year."

A good formula, but it will not work for valuation. You need your cash flows to fall at the end of the last projected year, not the beginning.

TERMINAL VALUE PROBLEMS

How much value is contained in the terminal value and how much in the projected period? It is hardly ever an even split. Usually about 60 – 80% of the company's value is in its terminal value. If you make a mistake in your terminal value calculation, your whole valuation will be seriously wrong. Below are some classic mistake-prone areas:

Cyclical companies

Cyclical companies never reach a steady state. They are always oscillating through their business cycle. To calculate steady state for a cyclical company, average its margins and investing requirements as a % of sales over its whole cycle. Calculate the terminal value free cash flow using your average numbers.

Unrealistic trends

The best way of forecasting the investing activities in the terminal year is to keep your key asset and liability items constant as a % of sales in the last two forecast years. Avoid embedding unrealistic trends in your forecast; for instance, showing net fixed assets and OWC growing or decreasing as a % of sales.

A small error in your forecast period is magnified many times over if it affects your terminal value calculation.

Capex versus depreciation

A common error is to make capital expenditure equal to depreciation in your final forecast year. If g is greater than zero in your terminal value assumptions, you will need to grow your net fixed assets to support the growth in the business. Keeping capex equal to depreciation keeps your net fixed assets constant, not growing.

Capex is the current year's replacement cost of assets; depreciation is the historical cost of assets spread into the future. If g includes inflation, the replacement cost (capex) should be larger than the historical cost (depreciation).

Banbury Bakeries Ltd

WACC	10.0%				
LT growth rate	3.0%				
					Steady state
	Y0	**Y1**	**Y2**	**Y3**	**Y4**
Free cash flow		65.0	80.0	112.0	115.0
Terminal value					1,692.1
Total cash flows		65.0	80.0	112.0	1,807.1

Formulas:

Terminal value

$$1{,}692.1 = \frac{115.0 * (1 + 3\%)}{(10\% - 3\%)}$$

The terminal value is the present value of a cash flow growing into perpetuity so you *do* apply a mid-year adjustment to the Gordon Growth Model terminal value.

THE VALUE DRIVER METHOD

In response to some of the problems presented by the Gordon Growth Model, analysts developed ***the value driver method***.

Changing the growth rate in the Gordon Growth Model

If a company starts to grow faster, its free cash flows fall in the short-term because the business requires more investment to support its growth. In the Gordon Growth Model, the growth rate, *g*, is not linked to the growth of fixed assets or operating working capital. If *g* increases, free cash flow stays constant instead of falling. You are getting the growth free and therefore overstating your valuation.

The difference between EBIAT and FCF effectively represents the net new investments the company is making.

The value driver method solves this problem.

Value driver formula

$$TV = \frac{EBIAT_{n+1} * \left(1 - \frac{g}{RONI}\right)}{(WACC - g)}$$

TV	Terminal value
EBIAT	Earnings before interest, after taxes
g	Long-term growth rate
RONI	Return on new investment

WACC Weighted average cost of capital

Diane

In your forecast of Diane Inc., your last projected year's EBIAT is 100. You forecast a terminal growth rate of 4% and a WACC of 9%. The return on new investment in the perpetuity period is 10%.

The top half of the value driver formula calculates the EBIAT that must be reinvested in the business and how much can be paid out to debt and equity holders.

Percentage of EBIAT to be reinvested: $\frac{\mathbf{g}}{\mathbf{RONI}} = \frac{\mathbf{4\%}}{\mathbf{10\%}} = \mathbf{40\%}$

With a growth rate of 4%, the company needs to reinvest 40% of EBIAT in the business.

(1 - 40%) = 60% = the percentage available to debt and equity holders.

$$1{,}200 = \frac{100 * \left(1 - \frac{4\%}{10\%}\right)}{(9\% - 4\%)}$$

Comparing Gordon Growth Model and Value Driver Method

Notice what happens when you increase the growth rate in the Gordon Growth Model. Your terminal value increases, but your free cash flow remains steady, implying that the company can grow without paying for the growth.

Gordon Growth Model		
G	4.0%	5.0%
WACC	9.0%	9.0%
Free cash flow	60.0	60.0
Terminal value	***1,200.0***	***1,500.0***

Now examine the same inputs processed through the Value Driver method. Growth increases by 1%, as in the Gordon Growth Model; but here free cash flow drops, reflecting the cost of reinvestment to support the growth. The terminal value grows, but at a lower rate, again reflecting the cost of reinvestment.

Value driver method		
EBIAT	100.0	100.0
G	4.0%	5.0%
RONI	10.0%	10.0%
% EBIAT reinvested	40.0%	50.0%
% EBIAT paid out	60.0%	50.0%
WACC	9.0%	9.0%
Free cash flow	60.0	50.0
Terminal value	***1,200.0***	***1,250.0***

DISCOUNTING

Now you are ready to calculate the present value of the forecast cash flows and terminal value. To discount the cash flows, use the Present Value formula:

$$\textbf{Present Value} = \frac{\textbf{Future Value}}{(1 + \textbf{Discount Rate})^{\textbf{No of periods}}}$$

CALCULATING THE PRESENT VALUE

Using a discount rate of 10% and a long-term growth rate of 3%, discount the free cash flows for Banbury Bakeries:

Future value	Calculation	Present value
65	65 ÷ (1+10%)1	59
80	80 ÷ (1+10%)2	66
112	112 ÷ (1+10%)3	84
Total		209

WHEN DOES THE COMPANY GENERATE FREE CASH FLOWS?

Every day the company operates it generates free cash flows. Each year's total free cash flow is built up slowly, day by day:

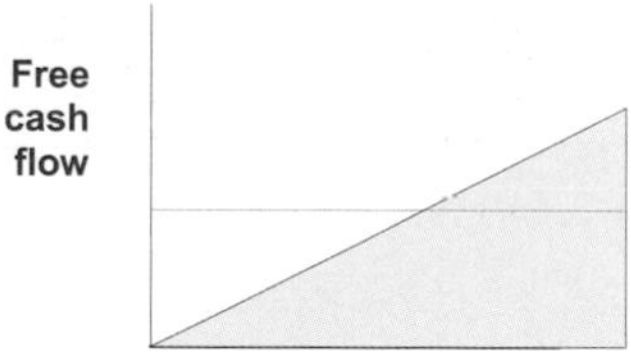

Free cash flow

Timing is everything

A company that sells Christmas trees receives most of its income near the last month of the year. Most companies, however, receive cash flows fairly evenly throughout the year. Another way of saying this is: the cash flows appear in the middle of the year on average.

When you discounted the cash flows above, the formula assumed they were generated at the end of each year. Oops! The cash flows are discounted by six months too much! This model works for the Christmas tree seller but not for most companies.

You should adjust the present value of the free cash flows forward by growing them by a half year:

$$219 = 209 * (1 + 10\%)^{0.5}$$

DISCOUNTING THE TERMINAL VALUE

You have three choices for calculating the terminal value:

- Enterprise Multiple method
- Gordon Growth Model
- Value Driver method

Although you make the half-year adjustment for the free cash flows in all methods, you must be careful how you handle the terminal value. The Gordon Growth Model and the Value Driver methods require you to make the half-year adjustment; the Enterprise Multiple method does not.

Enterprise multiple method: the exception

The multiple method gives you the value of the terminal value at the end of the last projected year. You are effectively assuming that you are selling the company at the end of the forecast horizon and receive the cash on a specific date. Do not make the mid-year adjustment if you use the multiple valuation method for your terminal value.

The multiple method does not use cash flows, so the mid-year rule does not apply to it. The multiple method gives you a one-time value for the business after your forecast period.

Do make the mid-year adjustment for your forecast free cash flows.

Mid-year adjustment

	Y0	Y1	Y2	Y3
EBIT		100.0	120.0	150.0
Tax at 20%		20.0	24.0	30.0
Free cash flow		65.0	80.0	112.0
Terminal value				1,650.0
Discount rate	10.0%			
Discount factor		90.9%	82.6%	75.1%
PV of cash flows		59.1	66.1	84.1
Total PV of cash flows	209.3			
Mid-year adjustment	219.5			
PV of terminal value	1,239.7			
Total Enterprise Value	1,459.2			

$$\textbf{Mid year adj} = 209.3 * (1 + 10\%)^{0.5} = 219.5$$

Gordon Growth Model and Value Driver Method

Both the Gordon Growth Model and Value Driver formula use cash flows not earnings to calculate the terminal value. They give you the amount of the terminal value in the ***middle*** of the last projected year. Make the mid-year adjustment for the terminal value in both these methods just as you would for the cash flows during the projection period.

Gordon Growth vs. Value Driver Methods

Using the Gordon Growth Model:

WACC	10.0%				
LT growth rate	3.0%				Steady
					state
	Y0	Y1	Y2	Y3	Y4
Free cash flow		65.0	80.0	112.0	115.0
Terminal value					1,692.1
Total cash flows		65.0	80.0	112.0	1,807.1
Discount factor		90.9%	82.6%	75.1%	68.3%
PV of total cash flows		59.1	66.1	84.1	1,234.3
Total PV of cash flows	1,443.6				
Mid year adjustment	1,514.1				

$$\textbf{Terminal Value} = \frac{115.0 \times (1 + 3\%)}{(10\% - 3\%)} = 1{,}692.1$$

Using the Value Driver Formula:

WACC	10.0%				
LT growth rate	3.0%				
Return on New Investment	11.0%				Steady
					state
	Y0	Y1	Y2	Y3	Y4
EBIAT					158.1
Free cash flow		65.0	80.0	112.0	115.0
Terminal value (value driver)					1,691.9
Total cash flows		65.0	80.0	112.0	1,806.9
Discount factor		90.90%	82.60%	75.10%	68.30%
PV of total cash flows		59.1	66.1	84.1	1,234.1
Total PV of cash flows	1,443.4				
Mid year adjustment	1,513.8				

$$\text{Terminal Value} = \frac{158.1 * (1 + 3\%) * \left(1 - \frac{3\%}{11\%}\right)}{(10\% - 3\%)} = 1{,}691.9$$

END RESULT

When you get the present value of the projected free cash flows and the terminal value, add them together to get enterprise value.

SPOT CHECK

A good practice is to discount the free cash flows during the projection period and the terminal value separately. You can then check the percentage of value from your projection period and compare it with the percentage of value from the terminal period. Spot checks help you spot errors.

Another good practice is to cross check your terminal value calculation using different methods. If you used the Gordon Growth Model calculate the implied Enterprise Multiple and vice versa. Use the equation below to do this:

$$\frac{EV}{EBIT} = \frac{FCF_n * (1 + g) * (1 + WACC)^{0.5}}{EBIT_n * (WACC - g)}$$

CALCULATING THE SHARE PRICE

Once you have the present value of the free cash flows and terminal value, you can calculate the share price. The present value of the projected free cash flows and terminal value gives you enterprise value.

THE SHARE PRICE CALCULATION

1. Start with enterprise value.
2. Calculate the equity value (equity value = enterprise value – net debt) by subtracting the value of the company's net debt at the date of valuation. If minority interests and preference shares are present, subtract them too.
3. Divide by the number of shares outstanding.

Banbury Bakeries Ltd

For this example assume:

- The Gordon Growth Model was used to calculate the terminal value's present value.
- Banbury Bakeries had 500 of debt and 50 of cash on its balance sheet.
- The market value of Banbury Bakeries debt was 450.
- Banbury Bakeries had 500 shares outstanding.

Total enterprise value:	1,514
Less market value of net debt	400
Equity value	1,114
Number of shares outstanding	500
Implied share price:	$2.23

WEIGHTED AVERAGE COST OF CAPITAL

When you valued Banbury Bakeries you were given a discount rate. The discount rate should reflect the riskiness of the cash flows you are discounting. For example, a large electricity company with relatively low risk would have a lower discount rate than a small airline with relatively high risk. The discount rate used in a Discounted Cash Flow Valuation is known as the weighted average cost of capital or WACC for short.

Another way of thinking about WACC is as the return investors require for risking their capital in that company.

THE CONCEPT OF RISK

All the financial markets measure risk by ***volatility***. In a DCF valuation, the risk lies in the volatility of the cash flows. The more a company's cash flows are likely to fluctuate, the higher the risk to investors. You reflect that higher risk by using a higher WACC in a DCF valuation.

WEIGHTED AVERAGE COST OF CAPITAL (WACC)

Most large companies use a combination of debt and equity to finance their assets. Their cost of capital is a combination of the cost of debt and the cost of equity. Large, stable companies with little risk of failure can raise debt and equity at a lower cost than small, struggling companies (higher risk companies).

In your attempt to get to one number that defines risk, you must weight the cost according to proportion of debt and equity in the company's capital structure. WACC is the combined, weighted cost of debt and equity. Here is the equation that defines WACC:

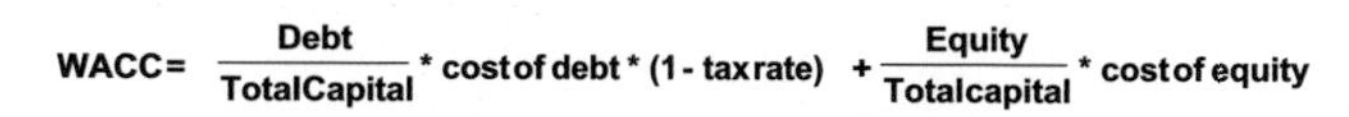

$$\text{WACC} = \frac{\text{Debt}}{\text{TotalCapital}} * \text{costof debt} * (1 - \text{taxrate}) + \frac{\text{Equity}}{\text{Totalcapital}} * \text{costof equity}$$

Debt	Usually pure debt, not net debt, at the date of valuation. Some analysts use net debt. Check with your firm. Pure debt advocates say net debt fluctuates too much because it includes surplus cash.
Total capital	Debt + equity at market value at the date of valuation.
Tax rate	Use the marginal tax rate, not the effective. The effective rate is an average tax rate. The marginal rate gives you the correct tax shield. Add the corporate tax rate plus any local income taxes to get the marginal rate. Note to US analysts: "Local" means national and state.

Cost of debt and equity. See detailed discussions below.

AFTER TAX COST OF DEBT

Notice that you use the after-tax cost of debt. Remember that the free cash flows did not include the effect of interest when you calculated tax. Most business do have debt and interest expenses. The WACC picks up the tax savings from interest payments.

Why put the tax savings from interest in WACC? The reason is practical. If you want to sensitize your model to changes in the capital structure (proportions of debt and equity), it is easier to change one WACC input than all five years of your projected cash flows. Without including the tax shield in WACC, you would have to project its impact in the free cash flow analysis.

PROPORTIONS OF DEBT AND EQUITY (CAPITAL STRUCTURE)

You must calculate the proportion of debt to equity to derive the WACC correctly. When calculating, use the market values of debt and equity. Your WACC defines a cost to the company but a return to the investor. Investors calculate their returns from market values, not book values.

You may encounter two situations in which you cannot use the company's market value of debt and equity: 1) the company is unlisted; 2) a one-time event like an acquisition has temporarily affected the capital structure. What can you do?

Companies in similar industries should have similar capital structures in an efficient market. Find a comparable and use its capital structure.

AN IMPORTANT NOTE

If you are valuing a subsidiary, calculate the cost of capital for the subsidiary, not the parent company.

Janty Inc

Use the following assumptions to calculate Janty's weighted average cost of capital:

Cost of equity:	11.0%
Cost of debt:	6.0%
Book value of debt	345.0
Market value of debt	340.0
Book value of equity	300.0
Market value of equity	345.0
Tax rate	30.0%
Ke	11.0%
Kd after tax	4.2%
% equity	50.4%
% debt	49.6%
WACC	7.6%

FINDING THE COST OF DEBT

You cannot just go to a company's annual report and capture their cost of debt for use in your WACC calculation. The cost of debt in the annual report is historical and may not reflect your choice of debt – equity mix in your WACC or the cost of debt in the future. You must find the company's future cost of debt for the credit rating implied by the debt-equity mix in your WACC.

First, determine the credit rating the company would have, given your assumed debt-equity mix. Standard and Poor's, Moody's, and other credit ratings services publish ratio guidelines for different credit ratings. The rating guides change frequently, so check for the latest information.

Once you have the credit rating, ask your capital markets or credit department for the cost of debt for that credit rating, or check Bloomberg for the yield on publicly traded long-term bonds with the same credit rating.

The difference between a company's cost of debt and the benchmark rate (usually LIBOR or a government bond) is called a spread. Bankers talk about spreads when discussing a company's cost of debt.

Inch Co

Inch Co's EBIT / interest ratio is rated as BBB. Looking at the graph below you establish the relevant cost of debt is 2% over the government bond rate.

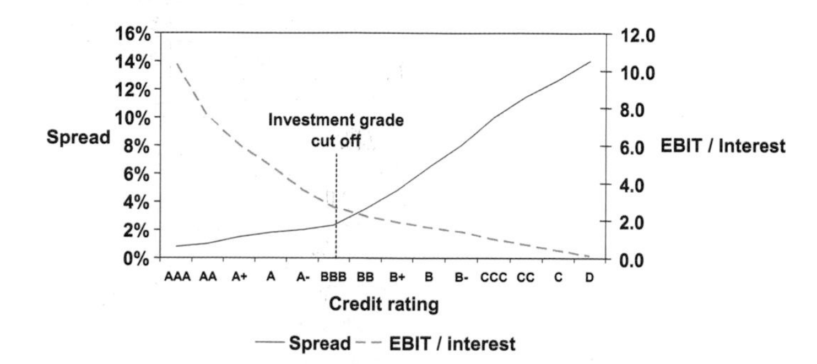

FINDING THE COST OF EQUITY

The most common method of calculating cost of equity is the Capital Asset Pricing Model (CAPM). CAPM is based on the theory that investors expect a greater return for taking more risk. CAPM divides the return investors expect into three elements:

Cost of equity = risk free rate + market risk premium x adjustment to reflect the company's risk profile (beta)

Risk free rate The return investors expect from a completely risk free investment. The "get out of bed money" for an investor. The closest approximation we have to the risk free rate is the yield on government bonds. Most bankers use the 10-year government bond.

Market risk premium Investing in the stock market is riskier than investing in government bonds. Investors expect a higher return to induce them to take the higher risk of investing in equities. The market risk premium prices the additional risk. Massive amounts of debate rage on what should be the correct market risk premium. Most bankers use between 4% and 6%. Check internally first to avoid any cat fights!

A STOCK'S RISK COMPARED TO THE MARKET'S RISK = BETA

The market risk premium works perfectly if a company has the same risk level as the market. In real life, such a situation almost never occurs. Companies have either higher or lower risk than the market in general. How do you measure the risk?

Volatility measures risk. A company whose stock price swings more widely up and down than the market is more volatile than the market and therefore more risky. A stock with more volatility than the market and therefore more risk will need the market risk premium adjusted upwards. Stocks with less volatility will need a downward adjustment.

The adjustment to the risk premium is called beta. Beta measures the volatility of the returns of a particular stock compared to the overall market returns. CAPM uses ***beta*** in its risk adjustment.

Suppose the return on the stock market as a whole increases by 10%.

- The stock price of a company with a beta of 1 will rise by 10%.
- The stock price of a company with a beta of 0.5 will rise by 5%.
- The stock price of a company with a beta of 2 will rise by 20%.

Industry Betas

Industry Name	Beta
Securities Brokerage	0.78
Cement & Aggregates	0.87
Retail Store	0.87
Precious metals	0.88
Entertainment	1.12
Telecom Services	1.15
Air Transport	1.17
Cable TV	1.35
Internet	2.46

WHAT RISKS DOES BETA MEASURE?

Non-systemic risks are risks specific to the firm, such as the risk of a major fire in a factory. *Systemic risks* are risks that affect all companies. Examples include the OPEC oil shock in 1974 and rises in interest rates.

CAPM assumes non-systemic risk can be diversified away by holding a range of stocks. Beta does not include non-systemic risks.

Once you have a company's beta you can complete the cost of equity and the Capital Asset Pricing Model.

Cost of equity = risk free rate + (market risk premium x beta)

Rizzo Ltd.

Rizzo's weighted average cost of capital:

Risk free rate	5.0%
Equity risk premium	4.0%
Beta	1.1
Market value of debt	532.0
Market value of equity	758.0
Cost of debt	6.5%
Tax rate	30.0%
Ke	9.4%
Kd after tax	4.6%
% of equity capital	58.8%
% of debt capital	41.2%
WACC	7.4%

THE IMPACT OF LEVERAGE ON BETA

When a company increases its debt to equity ratio, it also increases its interest expense, which is a fixed cost. The company's earnings after tax will fluctuate more when affected by systemic shocks than the earnings of a company with less leverage. Its stock price will also fluctuate more and its returns to shareholders will be more volatile. Higher volatility means more risk.

As a company takes on more debt, adjust its beta to account for the greater volatility of its returns. Use the following equation to adjust the company's *unlevered beta* (the company's beta if it were financed with 100% equity):

$$\text{Beta}_L = \text{Beta}_u * \left(1 + \frac{\text{debt}}{\text{equity}} * (1 - \text{marginal tax rate})\right)$$

Rearrange the formula to "unlever" a beta:

$$\text{Beta}_u = \frac{\text{Beta}_L}{\left(1 + \frac{\text{debt}}{\text{equity}} * (1 - \text{marginal tax rate})\right)}$$

THE UNLEVERED BETA

The unlevered beta is also known as the *asset beta*. It reflects the risk of investing in the company's assets. Debt and equity finance the assets and take on the risk inherent in the assets.

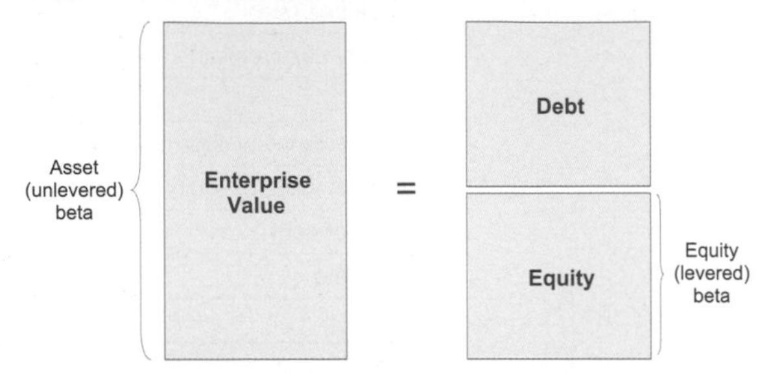

WHEN SHOULD YOU USE THE LEVERING AND UNLEVERING EQUATIONS?

You can find a beta for a company only when its stock is quoted. If your company is not quoted, you have a problem. Solve it by finding a comparable quoted company.

The problem is the comparable company may have a different capital structure and a levered beta inappropriate for your company. If they are good comparables, their unlevered betas should be very similar.

Calculate a suitable beta

Step 1. Unlever the comparable's beta using its existing capital structure.

Step 2. Re-lever the beta using your chosen, ongoing capital structure for the company you want to value.

Summary

- Use the company's target capital structure when re-levering your beta.
- Use market values of debt and equity.

Library

London Supermarket's Weighted Average Cost of Capital

- The current capital structure includes 40% equity and 60% debt. London Supermarket's target capital structure is 50% equity and 50% debt.
- The market risk premium is 4%.
- The 10 year government bond is currently yielding 5%.
- The current tax rate is 30%.
- London Supermarkets can currently raise debt at a rate of 7.0%.

You do not have an estimate of London Supermarket's beta. The closest comparable you can find is Finchley Food Markets which has a levered beta of 0.9. Finchley's latest balance sheet shows 300m debt and 400m of equity. Finchley's market capitalization (the market value of equity) is currently 600m.

Finchley's levered beta	0.90	
Finchley's unlevered beta	0.67	= 0.9 / (1 + 300 / 600 * (1 - 30%))
Relever the beta for London	1.14	= 0.67 * (1 + 50% / 50% * (1 - 30%))
Ke	9.6%	
Kd after tax	4.9%	
% debt	50.0%	
% equity	50.0%	
WACC	7.2%	

DCF Details

Yield Curve

The line produced when you line up all the yields (returns) from the shortest term to the longest term bond

THE RISK-FREE RATE

Definition

A completely risk-free security has no default risk, no volatility, and a beta of zero. You will not be able to find a security that meets all these requirements, so you must choose the next best thing: a security issued by a politically and economically stable government. However, academics have significant disagreements about the optimal period to maturity of the government security.

What did the origional inventors of CAPM use?

CAPM was originally devised to cover a one-year period. The maturity of the risk-free rate was not important in this early model. When you are using CAPM to value streams of cash flows to infinity, the period to maturity becomes a very real issue.

What are the choices and why is it important?

Using the US as an example, practitioners' choices range between the 3-month Treasury bill and a 30-year Treasury bond. About 80% of the time, the yield curve slopes upwards. Under this condition the 3-month Treasury bill gives you a lower result than the 30-year bond. 30-year bonds fluctuate in price much more widely than the 3-month bills and so require a volatility premium.

Between 1926 and 2002 the average (arithmetic) spread between long-term government bonds and US Treasury bills was approximately 150 basis points. Depending on the security you choose, your risk free cost of equity could vary by up to 1.5%.

Short-term rate or long-term rate?

3-month Treasury Bill

- More consistent with the original CAPM theory.
- Short-term rates change significantly over time. The long-term average of the 3-month Treasury bill would better approximate the real risk-free rate. Otherwise you might pick a peak or a trough.
- If the yield curve is upward, then long bonds get a higher return than 3-month T-bills. A higher return suggests the long bond is compensating investors for taking additional risk. Therefore the long bond is not completely risk-free.

Long-term government bonds•

- In a DCF, you forecast five to ten years into the future. Long bonds represent a better match with the maturity of the cash flows in your DCF.
- A long bond's yield includes a long-term forecast of inflation. A historical average of 3-month Treasury yields does not include an inflation forecast.
- Bonds are priced by discounting their future cash flows back to today. A change in the inflation rate has little impact on the price of a 3-month T-bill with only one future cash flow but a significant impact on the price of a 30-year Treasury bond with up to 60 cash flows. For the same change in inflation rate, the long bond will be much more volatile than the short-term Treasury bill. As you know, volatility equals risk in the financial markets. Therefore the 30-year bond is not completely risk-free.

Currency Swaps

**Overseas operations often create mismatches between financing currency & revenue currency. When McDonald's built outlets in Russia, it financed them with dollars but received roubles from its customers. McDonalds now runs the risk that the rouble will drop in value relative to the dollar. If McDonalds could swap dollar financing for rouble financing, it would face less risk. Currency swaps help reduce exposure to currency fluctuation risk.
The spread measures the risk of holding a foreign currency compared to the home currency.**

WHAT IS COMMONLY USED?

Most firms use a ten-year government bond from an economically and politically stable country.

ALTERNATIVES

A more complex and time-consuming method is to estimate the risk-free rate that applies to the maturity of each cash flow in your projection. You'll end up with a series of estimates, one for each cash flow. Use your estimates to recalculate WACC for every year of your forecast. Then recalculate the cost of capital for each year using each different WACC.

Forecasting the risk-free rate and recalculating the cost of equity every year involves a great deal more analysis.

WHAT IF YOU ARE VALUING A COMPANY FROM AN ECONOMICALLY AND POLITICALLY UNSTABLE COUNTRY?

The yield on government bonds from unstable countries can fluctuate wildly. They are hard to use in a valuation. An alternative is to take a stable country's 10-year bond and add a country risk premium to it. You can find the country risk premium from the spread on currency.

ESTIMATING THE EQUITY RISK

THE EQUITY RISK PREMIUM

The equity risk premium (also known as the market risk premium) is the additional return, over and above the risk-free rate investors expect for putting their money into the stock market.

There is no consensus about what the long-term equity risk premium should be; in fact, there is a good deal of disagreement. Do not believe people who say they have the definitive answer! Figures used by practitioners and academics range from 4.0% to in excess of 7.0% in the US market.

THE DIFFICULTY…

…is finding out what return investors expect from investing in the stock market. By definition, the equity risk premium is the difference between the expected return on the equity market and the risk-free rate.

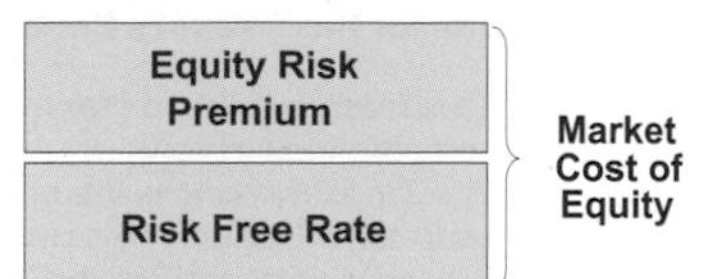

The arithmetic average assumes distribution of returns is stable over time and yearly returns are independent of each other. The geometric average measures the compounded rate of return. It is similar to the internal rate of return (IRR) calculation and implies investors buy and hold their market portfolio, reinvesting any dividends. Unless the returns are the same every year, the geometric average will give a lower result than the arithmetic average

Looking forward

One option is to look at historical returns to estimate future expectations. A common approach by academics is to take the average of the difference between the risk-free rate and the return on the stock market over the long-term.

Which average…

…arithmetic or geometric? Between 1919 and 1993 the difference between the arithmetic and geometric mean return of the UK stock market was 3%. The choice between the two average calculations is an important reason for different estimates of the equity risk premium, and academics can get highly exercised over these two views.

Arguments for arithmetic

- When you discount cash flows in your DCF, you use an arithmetic calculation.
- The geometric mean smoothes out the volatility of returns. However, the risk premium needs to capture the volatility to measure the risk to investors accurately.
- Discounting future cash flows in capital budgeting uses an arithmetic calculation.

Arguments for geometric

- The arithmetic average can be biased if you change the measurement period.
- The arithmetic average assumes yearly returns are "independent" (no effect on future trends). The geometric mean takes the historical path of returns and projects it forward.
- The geometric average is a better predictor of the average premium over the long-term.

Which government security?

Academics debate about which government security to use as a risk -free rate when calculating the equity risk premium. In the United States both Treasury bills and Treasury bonds are used. The choice between Treasury bills and Treasury bonds introduces another margin for error. Over the long-term the difference between Treasury bills and ten-year Treasury bonds averages 150 basis points.

Arguments for the Treasury Bill

- The Treasury bond is not completely risk-free; it has a small beta due to its higher volatility.
- The CAPM model is a one-period model of risk and return so a Treasury bill is more appropriate.

Arguments for the Treasury Bond

- The Treasury bond better matches the maturity of a company's cash flows.
- The Treasury bond is the geometric average of the expected short-term Treasury bills over the period.
- It is inconsistent to use the Treasury bill to help calculate the equity risk premium if you use the Treasury bond as the risk-free rate in CAPM.

Do the choices matter?

The four choices give very different results:

	T-Bill returns	T-Bond returns
Arithmetic mean	7.67%	6.25%
Geometric mean	5.73%	4.53%

Is there a consensus?

- Most practitioners take the view that the risk-free rate in the CAPM equation should match the maturity of the cash flows being valued. In order to ensure a match, analysts typically use a Treasury bond rate of approximately ten years.
- The majority of practitioners use the arithmetic mean of the difference between the Treasury bill rate and the return on the stock market to estimate the equity risk premium for the CAPM equation.

LOOKING FORWARD

An alternative way of calculating the cost of equity is to estimate the expected return on the market using the analysts' forecasts of the market's free cash flows to equity holders.

Remember the Gordon Growth Model equation:

$$\textbf{Market value} = \frac{\textbf{FCF to equity holders}}{\textbf{(cost of equity - g)}}$$

Rearrange the equation to help solve for the expected market return (the cost of equity):

$$\textbf{Market's cost of equity} = \frac{\textbf{FCF to equity holders}}{\textbf{market value}} + \textbf{g}$$

To calculate the equity risk premium, simply subtract the risk-free rate.

BETA

> **Covariance**
>
> **Covariance is a statistical measure that quantifies the amount by which the difference of the stock's return from its mean moves with the difference of the market's return from its mean. Alternatively the covariance is the product of three items: the correlation coefficient between the stock and the market, the standard deviation of the stock's return, and the market's return.**

DEFINITION

Beta measures the volatility of a stock compared to the volatility of the overall market. Calculate it by taking the covariance between the stock's return and the market's return.

HOW DO YOU INTERPRET BETA?

If a stock has a beta of 2 then, on average, for every 10% returned by the market (over the risk-free rate) the return on the stock will be 20%. If a stock has a beta of 0.5 then, on average, for every 10% returned by the market (over the risk-free rate) the return on the stock will be 5%. The relationship is effectively shown by the following graph.

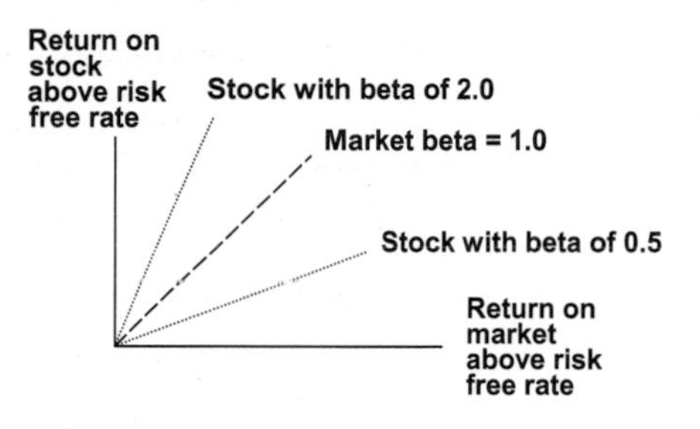

A stock with a beta of 2.0 has a much steeper line as its returns increase faster than the market. A stock with a beta of 0.5 has a shallower line as its returns increase more slowly than the market.

HOW IS BETA CALCULATED?

Beta is measured using regression techniques to analyze a stock's monthly returns over a substantial time period (usually three to five years). Beta is the *slope* of the line below:

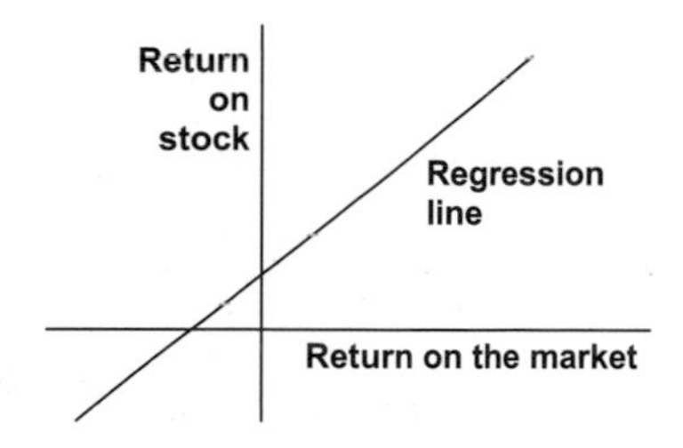

However, historical betas present problems in the Capital Asset Pricing Model:

- The regression for a particular stock's beta may not be very strong. Look at the standard deviation to determine the strength of the regression.
- Over a three to five year period the business can change quite dramatically. If the business changes then the volatility of earnings will change; so will the volatility of the stock.
- Betas are affected by leverage. Over three to five years a company's leverage will probably change.

USING BETAS IN CAPM

You use the Capital Asset Pricing Model to discount ***future*** cash flows. Betas calculated from the raw historical data (raw betas) are backward looking. Companies like Barra publish ***predicted*** betas which look forward not backward. Most analysts use predicted betas Always check the company's beta with its peer group's betas and the industry beta to "sanity check" your figure.

WHAT RISKS AFFECT A COMPANY'S BETA?

Beta measures volatility related only to systemic risk. Systemic risks are risks affecting the market as a whole, not just the individual firm.

Examples of systemic risks (included in beta)

- Interest rate moves
- Recessions and booms (the business cycle)
- Thermo-nuclear war

Examples of company-specific risks (not included in beta)

- A fire in a factory
- The CEO dying

Why does beta not include company specific risks?

Modern portfolio theory assumes asset managers can diversify away company specific risk. Their portfolios are so large that a single company event has an imperceptible impact on its overall return. If company-specific risk can be diversified away, then investors will not expect to be rewarded for it.

WHAT FACTORS INFLUENCE A COMPANY'S BETA?

Different companies react differently to systemic risks. Key factors influencing a company's beta include:

- The type of business a company is in. Cyclical firms are expected to have higher betas than non-cyclical firms.
- The level of operating leverage a company has. A firm with higher operating leverage will see more volatile earnings compared to a firm with lower operating leverage.
- The level of financial leverage a company has. A firm with higher financial leverage will have more volatile earnings compared to a firm with lower financial leverage.

Leverage is about fixed costs. You have two types of fixed costs: operating fixed costs, for example, the headquarters building, and financing fixed costs, for example, the interest on debt. Both types of fixed costs do not change with output. In other words, if sales increase, the headquarters building still costs the same, and the interest on debt stays fixed.

WHERE DO YOU FIND BETAS?

The betas of most publicly traded companies are calculated and published on a regular basis. Reputable institutions that do this include BARRA and Ibbotson Associates in the US, and the London Business School in the UK.

Does your beta look sensible?

The beta of the stock market is 1.0. A more volatile stock will have a higher beta and a less volatile stock will have a lower beta. Examples include:

Industry Name	Beta
Securities Brokerage	0.78
Cement & Aggregates	0.87
Retail Store	0.87
Precious Metals	0.88
Entertainment	1.12
Telecom Services	1.15
Air Transport	1.17
Cable TV	1.35
Internet	2.46

BETA AND LEVERAGE

A company that increases its financial leverage will see its beta rise. Look at the following example illustrating the higher earnings volatility created as a result of higher leverage.

	Pre i-rate inc		Post i-rate inc	
	High level	Low level	High level	Low level
EBIT	200	200	180	180
Int. expense	50	10	60	12
PBT	150	190	120	168
% decrease			(20%)	(12%)

When interest rates rise, interest expense for both firms rises by 20%. In tandem with the interest rate rise we see a fall in EBIT as a result of falling sales - related to the interest rate hike. The highly leveraged firm sees its profitability decrease by 20% compared to only 12% for the low leveraged firm.

ADJUSTING BETA FOR LEVERAGE

If you are valuing a company that you expect to change its capital structure, you should also change its beta. The following equations are used to unlever and relever beta.

$$\beta_u = \frac{\beta_L}{\left(1 + \left[\frac{debt}{equity} * (1 - t)\right]\right)}$$

$$\beta_L = \beta_u * \left(1 + \left[\frac{debt}{equity} * (1 - t)\right]\right)$$

COMPANIES WITHOUT PUBLISHED BETAS

If you are valuing a company with no published beta, choose a selection of close comparable companies with published betas. First, unlever the comparable companies' betas using their existing capital structure (remember to use market values). Then relever the average unlevered beta using the target capital structure of the company you want to value.

You should be extremely careful when choosing the average, if there is a high level of deviation between the peer group betas. The peer group may need to be narrowed down or, alternatively the median can be used in addition to the mean. It is also helpful to compare the betas to the "float" or percentage of shares which are freely floating. Small floats can lead to distortions in volatility.

Stockwell Grocers

You want to value Stockwell Grocers using CAPM. Stockwell has no published beta, but its close comparable Holloway Food stores does. You prepare the following information:

- Stockwell's target debt/equity ratio: 60%
- Holloway's market debt/equity ratio: 35%
- Holloway's predicted beta: 1.1
- Tax rate: 30%

Step 1

Unlever Holloway's predicted beta:

$$0.9 = \frac{1.1}{(1 + [35\% * (1 - 30\%)])}$$

Step 2

Relever the unlevered beta using Stockwell's target debt equity ratio:

$$1.3 = 0.9 * (1 + [60\% * (1 - 30\%)])$$

Step 3

You can now use a beta of 1.3 in Stockwell's CAPM equation.

RECENT CRITICISMS OF BETA

The Capital Asset Pricing Model has been subjected to heavy criticism in recent years. Much of the attention has centered on the use of beta to help determine a company's cost of equity.

In 1992 Eugene Fama and Ken French of Chicago University declared:

"In short, our tests do not support the most basic prediction of the SLB model [The Capital Asset Pricing Model] that average stock returns are positively related to market betas."

Fama and French went onto claim that size and market to book ratios are better indicators of likely returns. Fama and French's claim was contested by Amihud, Christensen and Mendelson (ACM). ACM used the same data, and various statistical methods do show that betas are good predictors of the returns of different stocks. However, they have also identified that betas do not explain stock returns post 1982.

WHY HAS THE RELATIONSHIP BETWEEN BETA AND RETURNS BROKEN DOWN?

Several arguments are put forward:

- Indexing (inclusion of top 100, 250 companies etc. in portfolios) has allowed larger, lower beta stocks in the S&P to outperform smaller higher beta stocks
- Increased stringency over inclusion of firms with limited floats in indices has distorted the relationship between beta and returns
- Investors may irrationally favor larger firms
- Investors may lack the resources to buy enough shares to diversify their risk completely

SHOULD YOU USE CAPM?

Despite the recent criticisms of beta and the problems of calculating the equity risk premium, CAPM is still the preferred model for calculating the cost of equity. In part, the widespread understanding of the CAPM has made practitioners reluctant to use a different model.

When using the CAPM model:

- Check your estimate of the company's cost of equity with an industry expert
- Run sensitivities on your discount rate if you are performing a corporate valuation

RETURN ON INVESTED CAPITAL (ROIC)

When valuing companies analysts need to be able to assess the company's performance in respect of profitability, growth and return. Returns can be calculated on an equity and invested capital basis. Return on equity is simply net income divided by shareholders' equity at book value. In order to assess the company's returns generated on all operating assets, ROIC is a more appropriate measure.

DEFINITION

Return on invested capital (ROIC) is an accounting-based measure of the cash return generated on capital invested in a company or business unit. It is a non-GAAP financial measure that quantifies how well a company generates cash flow relative to the capital it has invested in its business. ROIC is a one period measure of return and is usually expressed as a percentage.

THE CALCULATION

ROIC = Net operating profit after-tax (NOPAT)/invested capital (IC)

Where, in its simple form,

- NOPAT = Operating earnings after cash taxes, calculated as EBIT * (1-tax)
- Invested Capital = Total assets less excess cash minus non-interest bearing liabilities, alternatively net debt plus shareholders' equity at book value plus minority interest plus provisions.

ADJUSTING FOR ACCOUNTING DISTORTIONS

ROIC is usually thought of as a more accurate measurement of returns on capital invested because it can be adjusted for various accounting distortions. It also reflects returns that have been generating for *all* capital holders, including equity, debt, and preferred capital holders.

Common adjustments include the following (adjustments should be made in both the numerator and denominator of the equation):

- Capitalizing of operating leases
- Capitalizing and amortization of R&D costs
- Adjusting for various provisions/charge-offs and reserves

INTERPRETING ROIC

Generally speaking, the higher the level of ROIC, the more cash-generation power a company has. However, ROIC is even more informative when compared to a company's weighted average cost of capital (WACC) where the WACC represents the minimum require return by investors. Thus, the following value creation relationships exist:

- Value is created when ROIC > WACC
- Value is destroyed when ROIC < WACC
- Value is maintained (return generation = expectations) when ROIC = WACC

Using these relationships, it can further be said that value can be created by:

- Reallocating lower return-generating capital or improving the use of its existing capital to increase the spread between its ROIC and its cost of capital
- Investing more capital in the current business, as long as total ROIC stays above WACC
- Investing additional capital in new projects (outside of the traditional scope of the company's current businesses) that are expected to generate ROIC in excess of the WACC
- Lowering the WACC (increase debt or lower the risk profile of the asset base)
-

Looking at comparable company analysis we would expect companies with higher ROIC than their peers to trade at higher multiples.

Whilst performing a discounted cash flow analysis the measure of ROIC provides a useful tool for assessment of the terminal value assumptions. Furthermore, ROIC can be broken into its components (DuPont analysis):

$$\textbf{ROIC} = \frac{\textbf{EBIT}}{\textbf{Sales}} \times \frac{\textbf{Sales}}{\textbf{IC}} \times (\textbf{1} - \textbf{taxrate})$$

The first part of the equation represents the profitability of the company with the second part measuring the capital efficiency of the company. When forecasting the financials of a company analysts often spent very little time on the capital efficiency ratio which relates back to the investment rate as discussed above.

INTERPRETATION CAVEAT

It is important to not only look at the level of ROIC but also the trend. A high ROIC in a single period could signal strong management that has been successful at employing invested capital or it could indicate that management has sacrificed longer-term returns for current results.

In general, a company with increasing ROIC over time may Indicate management that is able to reinvest cash at higher rates of return. This may be seen, for example, in restructuring businesses.

Conversely, a company with declining ROIC over time may indicate management that is not able to invest additional capital in projects or businesses that generate returns above the company's WACC. This could be the case in an industry with excess competition and severe pricing pressures.

However, caveats have caveats. In rapidly growing companies (e.g. early stage growth companies), extremely high returns should be expected to decline over time as large amounts of capital are invested in the business. In this situation, the cash generation is creating value, while the percentage return is declining. This scenario only works when ROIC is significantly higher then WACC.

Limitations

Since ROIC is an accounting-based measure of return, it can suffer from several potential weaknesses, including the following:

- Manipulation by management
- Influence by accounting conventions and changes, particularly the treatment of R&D and marketing expenses
- The affect of inflation and currency exchange movements

Leveraged BuyOuts

1. BACKGROUND TO AN LBO AND WHAT COMPANIES MAKE GOOD LBO TARGETS

A leveraged buy-out is the acquisition of a target company primarily financed with debt collateralized by the target's cash flow (or in some cases its assets).

A company's value is derived by establishing how much a financial buyer could pay given two constraints:

- A target cost of equity
- The maximum sustainable leverage given the forecast cash flows

Financial buyers maximize their returns by purchasing companies using as much leverage as possible. They expect a high return on their equity usually between 20% and 35%.

Suitable companies for a LBO

Not all companies are suitable for an LBO. Good candidates should have the following characteristics:

- ***Good Management***; a highly geared company has little room for error at the operating level.
- ***Attractive Purchase Price***; usually the purchase price has to be attractive to generate the returns expected by investors.
- ***Stable cash flows***; an LBO has high fixed interest costs and capital repayments. It cannot support sudden fluctuations outside its cash flow forecast.
- ***Exit opportunities;*** typically LBO transactions are financed by Investors with a medium-term investment horizon (typically 3 to 5 years).
- ***Potential for operating Improvement;*** LBO investors may use cost improvements to generate their returns.
- ***Low capital expenditure requirements;*** most available cash flow is used for debt servicing. It is unlikely a LBO structure will support significant capital expenditure.

How LBOs increase shareholder value

LBO returns come from three key areas:

- The rise in shareholder value as debt is repaid with operational cash flow
- Margin improvement (increase) resulting in higher EBITDA, and therefore a higher enterprise value
- The tax shield on interest provided by the significant use of leverage

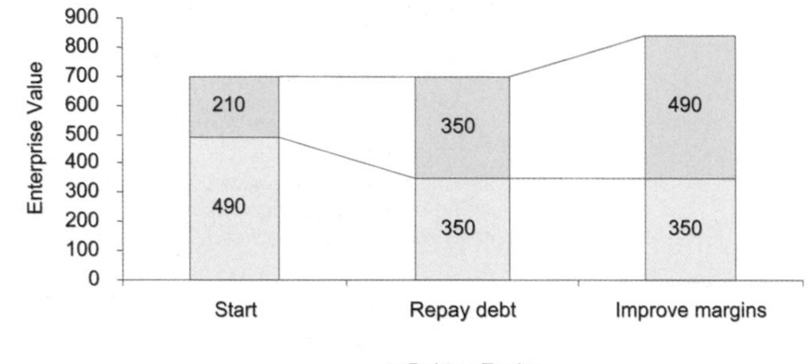

2. THE OPERATIONAL FORECAST

The LBO process starts with an operational forecast of a business's cash flows and earnings. Typically the forecast is prepared by the management team, or the private equity bidder. Your task is to "hang" a suitable financial structure onto the forecast. Key items in the forecast include:

Sales
EBIT
Depreciation
Amortization

Capital expenditure
Operating working capital items
Other operational assets and liabilities (if required)
Purchases of intangibles (if required)
Other investing items (if required)

You will also need to know

- Net debt at deal date
- Status of pension plan (if under funded)
- Other debt equivalents e.g. environmental or legal liabilities
- Outstanding options and their corresponding strike prices at deal date

The forecast allows you to establish both the debt capacity and the value of the firm in the exit year. Look at the operational forecast on the next page. The management team is expecting to improve the earnings and the cash flow generation of the business. Improving earnings helps generate extra cash flow and increases the Enterprise Value of the firm. More cash flow helps increase the debt capacity of the business.

The new management team will seek cost savings and will probably project a falling COGS % of sales ratio. Generates higher cash flow and an increased enterprise value as EBITDA rises.

SG&A also falls as the management team cut out uneccesary overhead costs. Generates higher cash flow and an increased enterprise value as EBITDA rises.

Receivables as a % of sales fall as the management team is more effective at collecting from customers. Reduced operating working capital improves cash flow.

Inventories as a % of COGS falls as the management team shorten the production cycle and implement just-in-time-inventory purchases. Reduced operating working capital improves cash flow.

Accounts payable as a % of COGS falls as the management team negotiates better terms with suppliers. Reduced operating working capital improves cash flow.

In most LBOs the firm is a cash generating mature business so sales growth is relatively low and stable.

Management forecast	*Hist*	*Proj*	*Proj*	*Proj*	*Proj*	*Proj*	*Proj*	*Proj*	*Proj*
Sales growth		5.00%	5.00%	5.00%	5.00%	5.00%	5.00%	5.00%	5.00%
COGS % of sales	(50.00%)	(49.50%)	(49.50%)	(49.50%)	(49.50%)	(49.50%)	(49.50%)	(49.50%)	(49.50%)
SG&A % of sales	(20.00%)	(19.00%)	(19.00%)	(19.00%)	(19.00%)	(19.00%)	(19.00%)	(19.00%)	(19.00%)
Depreciation % of prior year's net PP&E	(10.00%)	(10.00%)	(10.00%)	(10.00%)	(10.00%)	(10.00%)	(10.00%)	(10.00%)	(10.00%)
Receivables % sales	8.00%	7.50%	7.50%	7.50%	7.50%	7.50%	7.50%	7.50%	7.50%
Inventories % COGS	(6.80%)	(6.80%)	(6.50%)	(6.50%)	(6.50%)	(6.50%)	(6.50%)	(6.50%)	(6.50%)
Accounts payable % COGS	(6.00%)	(6.50%)	(6.50%)	(6.50%)	(6.50%)	(6.50%)	(6.50%)	(6.50%)	(6.50%)
Capital expenditure % sales	6.00%	3.00%	6.00%	6.00%	6.00%	6.00%	6.00%	6.00%	6.00%
Calculations									
Net PP&E									
Beginning balance	500.0	510.0	490.5	507.6	526.3	546.6	568.5	592.1	617.3
Capital expenditure	60.0	31.5	66.2	69.5	72.9	70.0	80.1	84.4	88.6
Depreciation	(50.0)	(51.0)	(49.1)	(50.8)	(52.6)	(54.7)	(56.9)	(59.2)	(61.7)
Ending balance	510.0	490.5	507.6	526.3	546.6	568.5	592.1	617.3	644.2
Income statement items									
Sales	1,000.0	1,050.0	1,102.5	1,157.6	1,215.5	1,276.3	1,340.1	1,407.1	1,477.5
COGS (excluding depreciation)	(500.0)	(519.8)	(545.7)	(573.0)	(601.7)	(631.8)	(663.3)	(696.5)	(731.3)
SG&A (excluding amortization)	(200.0)	(199.5)	(209.5)	(219.9)	(230.9)	(242.5)	(254.6)	(267.3)	(280.7)
EBITDA	300.0	330.8	347.3	364.7	382.9	402.0	422.1	443.2	465.4
Depreciation	(50.0)	(51.0)	(49.1)	(50.8)	(52.6)	(54.7)	(56.9)	(59.2)	(61.7)
EBIT	250.0	279.8	298.2	313.9	330.3	347.4	365.3	384.0	403.7
Interest expense	To be determined by new financial structure								
Income before tax	To be determined by new financial structure								
Tax expense	To be determined by new financial structure								
Net income	To be determined by new financial structure								
Balance sheet items									
Receivables	80.0	78.8	82.7	86.8	91.2	95.7	100.5	105.5	110.8
Inventories	34.0	35.3	35.5	37.2	39.1	41.1	43.1	45.3	47.5
Accounts payable	30.0	33.8	35.5	37.2	39.1	41.1	43.1	45.3	47.5
Operating working capital	84.0	80.3	82.7	86.8	91.2	95.7	100.5	105.5	110.8

In the early years the management team might reduce capex in the short term to help cash flow in the first year when debt repayment and interest demands are highest.

3. ESTABLISHING THE DEBT CAPACITY

One key to deciding how much a private equity house can pay for a business is establishing how much debt the business can support. Four issues influence debt capacity:

a. The amount of cash the business generates

b. The stability of the cash flows

c. The conditions in the financing market

d. The availability of assets for security

A. CASH GENERATION

High cash generative businesses tend to be slow growth and in mature industries. Cash generation is driven by:

a. Profitability

b. How much of the profits are reinvested back into the business

Take a look at two different examples of companies free cash flows:

	Mature business		Fast growth business	
Sales	1,000.0	1,050.0	1,000.0	1,200.0
EBIT	200.0	210.0	150.0	170.0
Tax rate	30.0%	30.0%	30.0%	30.0%
Working capital	150.0	158.0	150.0	180.0
Capex	(100.0)	(105.0)	(100.0)	(120.0)
Depreciation	90.0	94.0	90.0	100.0
NOPAT		147.0		119.0
Depreciation		94.0		100.0
(Capex)		(105.0)		(120.0)
(Inc) dec in working capital		(8.0)		(30.0)
Free cash flow		128.0		69.0
% of after tax profits paid out		87.1%		58.0%

The mature business pays out nearly all of the available after-tax profits. The fast growing business must reinvest approximately 42% of the profits in the business to fuel growth. The debt capacity of the mature business will be much higher. Let's assume banks will give the business a seven year loan at 7% pre-tax interest. Assuming all the free cash flow is paid out as either, interest or debt repayment, the following valuations may be calculated:

Mature business	Year 0	Year 1	Year 2	Year 3	Year 4	Year 5	Year 6	Year 7
NOPAT	147.0	209.5	219.9	230.9	242.5	254.6	267.3	280.7
Depreciation	94.0	99.2	104.2	109.4	114.9	120.6	126.6	133.0
(Capex)	(105.0)	(110.3)	(115.8)	(121.6)	(127.6)	(134.0)	(140.7)	(147.7)
(Inc) dec in working capital	(8.0)	(7.4)	(8.3)	(8.7)	(9.1)	(9.6)	(10.1)	(10.6)
Free cash flow	128.0	191.1	200.1	210.1	220.6	231.6	243.2	255.4
% of after tax profits paid out	87.1%	91.2%	91.0%	91.0%	91.0%	91.0%	91.0%	91.0%
Cost of debt pre-tax	7.0%							
Cost of debt post-tax	4.9%							
Net present value of cash flows	1,275.8							

Fast growing business	Year 0	Year 1	Year 2	Year 3	Year 4	Year 5	Year 6	Year 7
NOPAT	119.0	163.3	196.0	235.1	282.2	338.6	406.3	487.6
Depreciation	100.0	136.3	163.5	196.2	235.4	282.5	339.0	406.8
(Capex)	(120.0)	(164.2)	(197.0)	(236.4)	(283.7)	(340.4)	(408.5)	(490.2)
(Inc) dec in working capital	(30.0)	(66.2)	(49.2)	(59.1)	(70.9)	(85.1)	(102.1)	(122.5)
Free cash flow	69.0	69.1	113.2	135.9	163.0	195.6	234.8	281.7
% of after tax profits paid out	58.0%	42.3%	57.8%	57.8%	57.8%	57.8%	57.8%	57.8%
Cost of debt pre-tax	7.0%							
Cost of debt post-tax	4.9%							
Net present value of cash flows	952.9							

The mature business has a higher present value of cash flows (discounted by the after-tax cost of debt) which translates into a higher debt capacity, despite the higher after-tax profits in the fast growing company example.

B. Stability of cash flows

Leverage buy out structures typically finance approximately 70% to 75% of the purchase price by debt. The business cannot afford to miss an interest or principal repayment (called a technical default). The more stable and certain the cash flows, the less likelihood of default and the greater willingness of debt holders (banks) to support the higher leverage.

Businesses with stable cash flows normally have the following characteristics:

1. ***Strong competitive advantage.*** The existence of strong barriers to entry makes the business less prone to competitive threats. Competitive threats tend to push down prices and margins and reduce cash flows.

2. ***Staple product***. Companies with repeat-business staple products will be less affected by recessions. For example, even in a recession you have to buy food. A cyclical business is more likely to be affected by a recession which means it may not be able to make the agreed interest and principal repayments.

3. ***Stable technology and long product life cycle***. Industries with stable, proven technology are less likely to experience sudden changes in production techniques which can require significant investment and alter the competitive landscape.

4. ***Little client or industry concentration***. Companies with a diverse range of clients are less exposed to the loss of a major client to a competitor, or economic problems in one specific market sector.

C. Debt Structuring

Debt structuring - cash flow method

Traditionally the debt capacity of a business is measured by matching the debt repayments with the management cash flow forecast. Senior debt (normally Term A, B, and C) is typically structured around the cash flow forecast:

1. Term A: 7 year amortizing loan priced at 175 to 225 basis points above LIBOR
2. Term B: 8 year bullet repayment loan priced at 225 to 275 basis points above LIBOR
3. Term C: 9 year bullet repayment loan priced at 275 to 325 basis points above LIBOR

The most senior loan always should be paid off first (hence Term A is repaid before Term B and C). Taking our existing cash flow forecast we can establish the debt capacity based on just Term A financing at 7.0% pre-tax.

Free cash flows		*Year 1*	*Year 2*	*Year 3*	*Year 4*	*Year 5*	*Year 6*	*Year 7*
Tax rate		30.0%	30.0%	30.0%	30.0%	30.0%	30.0%	30.0%
NOPAT		195.8	208.8	219.7	231.2	243.2	255.7	268.8
Depreciation		51.0	49.1	50.8	52.6	54.7	56.9	59.2
Capital expenditure		(31.5)	(66.2)	(69.5)	(72.9)	(76.6)	(80.4)	(84.4)
(Inc) dec in OWC		3.7	(2.4)	(4.1)	(4.3)	(4.6)	(4.8)	(5.0)
Free cash flow		219.0	189.3	196.9	206.5	216.7	227.4	238.6
Term A								
Cost of debt pre-tax	7.0%							
Cost of debt post-tax	4.9%							
Total term A	1,233.8							

To increase the debt capacity we can extend the borrowing by structuring Term B to be repaid as a bullet in year 8. Of course, the bank will charge us more as Term B is paid off after Term A.

Free cash flows		*Year 1*	*Year 2*	*Year 3*	*Year 4*	*Year 5*	*Year 6*	*Year 7*	*Year 8*
Tax rate		30.0%	30.0%	30.0%	30.0%	30.0%	30.0%	30.0%	30.0%
NOPAT		195.8	208.8	219.7	231.2	243.2	255.7	268.8	282.6
Depreciation		51.0	49.1	50.8	52.6	54.7	56.9	59.2	61.7
Capital expenditure		(31.5)	(66.2)	(69.5)	(72.9)	(76.6)	(80.4)	(84.4)	(88.6)
(Inc) dec in OWC		3.7	(2.4)	(4.1)	(4.3)	(4.6)	(4.8)	(5.0)	(5.3)
Free cash flow		219.0	189.3	196.9	206.5	216.7	227.4	238.6	250.4
Term B									
Cost of debt pre-tax	7.5%								
Cost of debt post-tax	5.3%							237.9 * (1+5.3%)	
Interest on Term B		(12.5)	(12.5)	(12.5)	(12.5)	(12.5)	(12.5)	(12.5)	(12.5)
Total term B								250.4 ÷ (1 + 5.3%)	(237.9)
Cash available to support Term A		206.5	176.8	184.4	194.0	204.2	214.9	226.1	0.0
Term A									
Cost of debt pre-tax	7.0%								
Cost of debt post-tax	4.9%								
Total term A	1,161.3								
Total debt	1,399.2								
Total debt / EBITDA	4.7x								

The Term B principle is paid off in year 8. The interest on Term B is paid in cash annually, causing an additional drain on the cash flows between year 1 and 7. There is less cash available for Term A, and hence a lower amount of Term A can be raised. In total the debt capacity is raised as the amount of Term A + Term B combined (1,399.2 m) is higher than, just Term A in the first example (1,233.8 m). Remember, Term A still has a priority claim, above that of Term B with respect to cash flows.

The further you are able to extend the debt repayment the more future cash flow you are using to pay for the business today.

By issuing Term C, payable in year 9, we can extend the debt capacity even further.

Free cash flows		*Year 1*	*Year 2*	*Year 3*	*Year 4*	*Year 5*	*Year 6*	*Year 7*	*Year 8*	*Year 9*
Tax rate		30.0%	30.0%	30.0%	30.0%	30.0%	30.0%	30.0%	30.0%	30.0%
NOPAT		195.8	208.8	219.7	231.2	243.2	255.7	268.8	282.6	297.0
Depreciation		51.0	49.1	50.8	52.6	54.7	56.9	59.2	61.7	64.4
Capital expenditure		(31.5)	(66.2)	(69.5)	(72.9)	(76.6)	(80.4)	(84.4)	(88.6)	(93.1)
(Inc) dec in OWC		3.7	(2.4)	(4.1)	(4.3)	(4.6)	(4.8)	(5.0)	(5.3)	(5.5)
Free cash flow		219.0	189.3	196.9	206.5	216.7	227.4	238.6	250.4	262.8
Term C										
Cost of debt pre-tax	8.0%									
Cost of debt post-tax	5.6%								248.8 * (1 + 5.6%)	
Interest on Term C		(13.9)	(13.9)	(13.9)	(13.9)	(13.9)	(13.9)	(13.9)	(13.9)	(13.9)
Total term C									262.8 ÷ (1 + 5.6%)	(248.8)
Cash available to support Term B		205.1	175.4	183.0	192.6	202.7	213.4	224.6	236.4	0.0
Term B										
Cost of debt pre-tax	7.5%									
Cost of debt post-tax	5.3%									
Interest on Term B		(11.8)	(11.8)	(11.8)	(11.8)	(11.8)	(11.8)	(11.8)	(11.8)	
Total term B									(224.6)	
Cash available to support Term A		193.3	163.6	171.2	180.8	191.0	201.6	212.8	0.0	
Term A										
Cost of debt pre-tax	7.0%									
Cost of debt post-tax	4.9%									
Total term A	1,084.4									
Total debt	1,557.9									
Total debt / EBITDA	5.2x									

Each time another level of debt is layered onto the structure the debt capacity expands. By adding Term C the debt capacity has expanded to 1,557.9 m.

We can extend the debt capacity even further by taking the repayment to year 10 by issuing a PIK or Paid In Kind instrument. The most common form of PIK instrument is a mezzanine loan. Typically a mezzanine loan has warrants (options) attached to the security. The loan must be repaid, but the warrants can convert into ordinary shares. The conversion usually happens when the business is sold. From a debt capacity point of view a PIK note is a great way of increasing debt capacity as the interest is "rolled up" onto the balance of the loan rather than being paid in cash. In some jurisdictions the interest can also have a tax deduction when accruing the interest.

Free cash flows		*Year 1*	*Year 2*	*Year 3*	*Year 4*	*Year 5*	*Year 6*	*Year 7*	*Year 8*	*Year 9*	*Year 10*
Tax rate		30.0%	30.0%	30.0%	30.0%	30.0%	30.0%	30.0%	30.0%	30.0%	30.0%
NOPAT		195.8	208.8	219.7	231.2	243.2	255.7	268.8	282.6	297.0	312.1
Depreciation		51.0	49.1	50.8	52.6	54.7	56.9	59.2	61.7	64.4	67.3
Capital expenditure		(31.5)	(66.2)	(69.5)	(72.9)	(76.6)	(80.4)	(84.4)	(88.6)	(93.1)	(97.7)
(Inc) dec in OWC		3.7	(2.4)	(4.1)	(4.3)	(4.6)	(4.8)	(5.0)	(5.3)	(5.5)	(5.8)
Free cash flow		219.0	189.3	196.9	206.5	216.7	227.4	238.6	250.4	262.8	275.8
Term C											
Cost of debt pre-tax	8.0%										
Cost of debt post-tax	5.6%								248.8 * (1 + 5.6%)		
Interest on Term C		(13.9)	(13.9)	(13.9)	(13.9)	(13.9)	(13.9)	(13.9)	(13.9)	(13.9)	
Total term C									262.8 ÷ (1 + 5.6%)	(248.8)	
Cash available to support Term B		205.1	175.4	183.0	192.6	202.7	213.4	224.6	236.4	0.0	
Term B											
Cost of debt pre-tax	7.5%										
Cost of debt post-tax	5.3%										
Interest on Term B		(11.8)	(11.8)	(11.8)	(11.8)	(11.8)	(11.8)	(11.8)	(11.8)		
Total term B									(224.6)		
Cash available to support Term A		193.3	163.6	171.2	180.8	191.0	201.6	212.8	0.0		
Term A											
Cost of debt pre-tax	7.0%										
Cost of debt post-tax	4.9%										
Total term A	1,084.4										
PIK note											
Cost of debt pre-tax	9.0%										
Cost of debt post-tax	6.3%	=275.8 ÷ (1 + 6.3%)^10									
Total PIK note	149.7										275.8
Total debt	1,707.6										
Total debt / EBITDA	5.7x										

By taking a PIK note in year 10, the debt capacity is increased even further to a total of 1,707.6 m.

High Yield bonds are also used for ten-year financing packages, although they are not usually structured as PIK instruments. They normally have cash interest (occasionally they may be PIK or a cash/PIK toggle, where the company pays cash interest if it has spare cash) and a five year call option to pay off the bond early.

Other funding choices

So far we have concentrated on the traditional debt financing products. A Leveraged Buy Out structure could also include other financial instruments, such as:

Second lien

Second Lien is a relatively new source of financing, which evolved as a result of a weak mezzanine market. The lender only gets what is left over after the first ranking charge (normally the term loans) has been satisfied. Structured with a floating rate (LIBOR + 500bps), year 9.5 bullet repayment, a second-lien loan helps extend secured debt and therefore improves overall cost of funding. The maximum amount of funding is usually approximately €500m (up to about 0.75x EBITDA). Hedge funds are significant investors in Second Lien.

Mezzanine

Mezzanine is an "in between" source of financing between debt and equity as an alternative to high yield. Structured as a loan, sometimes with warrants (options) attached, with a spread of 500bps paid in cash, plus 500bps PIK over LIBOR (these are approximations and will change with the strength of the market). Mezzanine is priced with an internal rate of return of approximately 12% to 16%, and normally has a bullet repayment in year 10.

High yield

High yield bonds are generally unsecured obligations, with senior or subordinated ranking and a BB+ or below credit rating. They are normally fixed rate instruments with no maintenance covenants, a 10 year maturity and a 5 year call option to the company. Currently priced at between 6% and 9% per year, high yield has a normal maximum funding of €1bn (although some recent deals have raised more).

So far we have focused exclusively on cash flow lending. The debt capacity is dependent on the ability of the firm to generate cash. Now we will look at situations where we can structure financing beyond the traditional ten-year cash flow financing.

Extending debt capacity beyond ten years

Securitization and sale and lease back

Bankers can extend the financing even further than 10 years by using assets which can either be:

1. Securitized or,
2. Sold and leased back to the company

The company sells assets to a Special Purpose Vehicle (SPV) which finances the purchase by selling bonds securitized against the assets purchased. The company receives cash and has to pay the SPV a fee for the use of the assets. A sale and leaseback transaction is similar. The company sells the assets to a leasing firm and then rents them back. Under securitization or sale and lease backs the investors supporting the scheme are willing to take on much longer financing periods than 10 years. Securitization or sale and lease backs allow the private equity house to utilize cash flows beyond the traditional ten years to finance the purchase of the business.

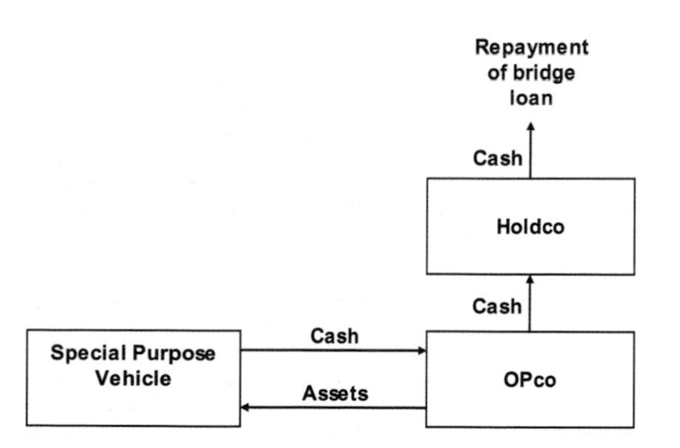

Refinancing risk

In recent years some leveraged buy out deals have been financed by investors accepting **"refinancing risk".** Instead of relying on the ability of the business to repay the debt using cash flow during the traditional ten-year period, investors are expecting the company to be able to refinance the principle on the repayment date with new debt.

Free cash flows		*Year 1*	*Year 2*	*Year 3*	*Year 4*	*Year 5*	*Year 6*	*Year 7*	*Year 8*	*Year 9*	*Year 10*
Tax rate		30.0%	30.0%	30.0%	30.0%	30.0%	30.0%	30.0%	30.0%	30.0%	30.0%
NOPAT		195.8	208.8	219.7	231.2	243.2	255.7	268.8	282.6	297.0	312.1
Depreciation		51.0	49.1	50.8	52.6	54.7	56.9	59.2	61.7	64.4	67.3
Capital expenditure		(31.5)	(66.2)	(69.5)	(72.9)	(76.6)	(80.4)	(84.4)	(88.6)	(93.1)	(97.7)
(Inc) dec in OWC		3.7	(2.4)	(4.1)	(4.3)	(4.6)	(4.8)	(5.0)	(5.3)	(5.5)	(5.8)
Free cash flow		219.0	189.3	196.9	206.5	216.7	227.4	238.6	250.4	262.8	275.8
Term C											
Cost of debt pre-tax	8.0%										
Cost of debt post-tax	5.6%										
Interest on Term C		(28.0)	(28.0)	(28.0)	(28.0)	(28.0)	(28.0)	(28.0)	(28.0)	(28.0)	
Total term C										(500.0)	
Cash available to support Term B		191.0	161.3	168.9	178.5	188.7	199.4	210.6	222.4	(265.2)	
Term B											
Cost of debt pre-tax	7.5%										
Cost of debt post-tax	5.3%										
Interest on Term B		(11.1)	(11.1)	(11.1)	(11.1)	(11.1)	(11.1)	(11.1)	(11.1)		
Total term B									(211.3)		
Cash available to support Term A		179.9	150.2	157.8	167.4	177.6	188.3	199.5	0.0		
Term A											
Cost of debt pre-tax	7.0%										
Cost of debt post-tax	4.9%										
Total term A	1,006.8										
PIK note											
Cost of debt pre-tax	9.0%										
Cost of debt post-tax	6.3%										
Total PIK note	217.1										400.0
Total debt	1,935.2										
Total debt / EBITDA	6.5x										

Refinancing risk analysis	*Year 1*	*Year 2*	*Year 3*	*Year 4*	*Year 5*	*Year 6*	*Year 7*	*Year 8*	*Year 9*	*Year 10*
Free cash flow	219.0	189.3	196.9	206.5	216.7	227.4	238.6	250.4	262.8	275.8
Term A interest and repayment	(179.9)	(150.2)	(157.8)	(167.4)	(177.6)	(188.3)	(199.5)	0.0	0.0	0.0
Term B interest and repayment	(11.1)	(11.1)	(11.1)	(11.1)	(11.1)	(11.1)	(11.1)	(222.4)	0.0	0.0
Term C interest and repayment	(28.0)	(28.0)	(28.0)	(28.0)	(28.0)	(28.0)	(28.0)	(28.0)	(528.0)	0.0
PIK note redemption	0.0	0.0	0.0	0.0	0.0	0.0	0.0	0.0	0.0	(400.0)
Surplus cash (refinancing risk where negative)	0.0	0.0	0.0	0.0	0.0	0.0	0.0	0.0	(265.2)	(124.2)

Where surplus cash is negative, the deal will face refinancing risk. In the above example, refinancing risk exists due to the negative surplus cash at the bottom of the repayment analysis.

Debt structuring - quick method

A faster way of establishing a company's debt capacity is to use industry standard multiples based on similar deals in comparable sectors. Capital markets bankers often have benchmark EBITDA multiples for certain sectors which they will use as rules of thumb:

Example multiples:

	EBITDA multiple
Term A	3.3x
Term B	3.9x
Term C	4.7x
PIK note	5.1x

So if a company's EBITDA is 300m you would structure a deal using the multiples above as a proxy for the cash flow analysis.

	EBITDA	multiple
Term A	1,084.4	3.3x
Term B	224.6	3.9x
Term C	248.8	4.7x
PIK note	149.7	5.1x

The quick method can be dangerous if the cash conversion profile of the company you are analyzing is not consistent with the general sector.

Summary financing terms

Typical current multiples include:

Senior debt (including second Lien) 3.5x to 4.0x

Mezzanine up to approximately €500m

High yield bonds up to approximately €1,000m

4. INITIAL DEAL STRUCTURE

Once you have established a suitable debt capacity you can put together an initial deal structure using some reasonable assumptions:

Key assumptions	
Share price	8.0
Acquisition premium	33.0%
Acquisition share price	10.6
Diluted shares outstanding	200.0
Acquisition equity price	2,128.0
Existing net debt	300.0
Acquisition Enterprise Value	2,428.0
EBITDA (latest historic or LTM)	300.0
Acquisition EV/EBITDA multiple	8.1x
Debt issuance fees % debt financing	2.0%
Advisors fees % of enterprise value	0.5%

		Cash flow analysis		EBITDA Multiple	% funding
Acquisition equity value	2,128.0	Term A	1,084.4	3.6x	43.8%
Refinanced net debt	300.0	Term B	224.6	4.4x	9.1%
Debt fees	34.2	Term C	248.8	5.2x	10.1%
Advisor fees	12.1	PIK note	149.7	5.7x	6.1%
		Equity (plug)	766.7	8.2x	31.0%
Total uses of funds	2,474.3	Total sources of funds	2,474.3		

The existing net debt will normally be refinanced as part of the deal, as change of control covenants will be triggered. Arrangement fees will be paid to the banks, and advisory fees will be paid to investment bankers, accountants, and lawyers.

The equity financing is a "plug". The debt capacity is agreed with the financing banks. If the private equity fund needs to pay more for the business they must put up the money.

Structural subordination

In the larger buy-outs the financing is structured in a tiered set of holding companies. The senior debt holders end up being closest to the operating cash flows. Dividends are paid up to the holding companies (inter group dividends are not taxed in most jurisdictions) to service the subordinated financing.

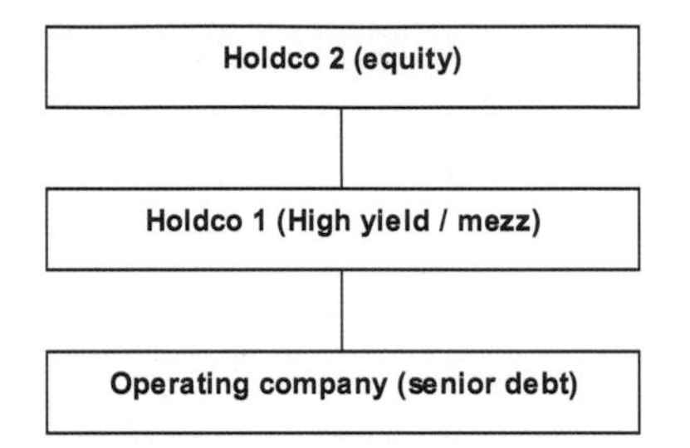

5. CALCULATING RETURNS TO EQUITY HOLDERS

Finally, we can calculate the returns to the equity holders using the initial structure. We expect the private equity house to sell the business within 3 to 5 years of the deal. Debt providers are downside-focused and although the debt funding may well be refinanced at the time of sale, we still assume the structure must pay down the debt. Using a reasonable transaction multiple (not higher than the original purchase multiple) we value the business between years 3 and 5, and then back out the equity value.

	Year 0	*Year 1*	*Year 2*	*Year 3*	*Year 4*	*Year 5*
EBITDA	300.0	330.8	347.3	364.7	382.9	402.0
Exit multiple	7.4x	7.4x	7.4x	7.4x	7.4x	7.4x
Enterprise value		2,447.6	2,569.9	2,698.4	2,833.3	2,975.0
Term A balance		944.3	827.0	696.3	549.7	385.6
Term B balance		224.6	224.6	224.6	224.6	224.6
Term C balance		248.8	248.8	248.8	248.8	248.8
PIK note balance		159.1	169.2	179.8	191.2	203.2
Equity value		870.6	1,100.3	1,348.8	1,619.0	1,912.7
Equity cash flows year 5 exit	(766.7)	0.0	0.0	1,348.8	0.0	0.0
IRR	20.7%					
Equity cash flows year 5 exit	(766.7)	0.0	0.0	0.0	0.0	1,912.7
IRR	20.1%					

Normally investors will expect a return to equity holders of at least 20% (sometimes lower or higher depending on the risk profile of the company concerned). In a competitive auction process the private equity buyers will bid the price of the company up until the returns fall to around 20%.

Share price	8.0
Acquisition premium	33.0%
Acquisition share price	10.6
Diluted shares outstanding	200.0
Acquisition equity price	2,128.0
Existing net debt	300.0
Acquisition Enterprise Value	2,428.0
EBITDA (latest historic or LTM)	300.0
Acquisition EV/EBITDA multiple	8.1x
Debt issuance fees % debt financing	2.0%
Advisors fees % of enterprise value	0.5%

		Cash flow analysis		EBITDA Multiple	% funding
Acquisition equity value	2,128.0	Term A	1,084.4	3.6x	43.8%
Refinanced net debt	300.0	Term B	224.6	4.4x	9.1%
Debt fees	34.2	Term C	248.8	5.2x	10.1%
Advisor fees	12.1	PIK note	149.7	5.7x	6.1%
		Equity (plug)	766.7	8.2x	31.0%
Total uses of funds	2,474.3	Total sources of funds	2,474.3		

Term A							
Beginning balance		1,084.4	944.3	827.0	696.3	549.7	385.6
Interest		53.1	46.3	40.5	34.1	26.9	18.9
Repayment and interest payment		(193.3)	(163.6)	(171.2)	(180.8)	(191.0)	(201.6)
Ending balance	1,084.4	944.3	827.0	696.3	549.7	385.6	202.9

	Year 0	*Year 1*	*Year 2*	*Year 3*	*Year 4*	*Year 5*	*Year 6*
EBITDA	300.0	330.8	347.3	364.7	382.9	402.0	422.1
Exit multiple	7.4x	7.4x	7.4x	7.4x	7.4x	7.4x	7.4x
Enterprise value		2,447.6	2,569.9	2,698.4	2,833.3	2,975.0	3,123.8
Term A balance		944.3	827.0	696.3	549.7	385.6	202.9
Term B balance		224.6	224.6	224.6	224.6	224.6	224.6
Term C balance		248.8	248.8	248.8	248.8	248.8	248.8
PIK note balance		159.1	169.2	179.8	191.2	203.2	216.0
Equity value		870.6	1,100.3	1,348.8	1,619.0	1,912.7	2,231.4
Equity cash flows year 5 exit	(766.7)	0.0	0.0	1,348.8	0.0	0.0	
IRR	20.7%						
Equity cash flows year 5 exit	(766.7)	0.0	0.0	0.0	0.0	1,912.7	
IRR	20.1%						

6. SENSITIZING THE STRUCTURE

Finally, both the operational forecast and the financial structure are sensitized. Usually three sets of operational assumptions are created:

- Base case
- Management case (most optimistic)
- Bank case (least optimistic)

The base case will normally show adequate returns to the private equity investors and easily meeting the debt servicing requirements. The bank case will normally show the bank still being repaid, but inadequate returns to equity holders.

The financial assumptions will be sensitized around the purchase price and the funding structure. The final structure is heavily dependent upon the investor appetite for different funding tranches. Refer to the example sensitivity analysis below.

Acquisition premium	Yr 3 IRR	Yr 5 IRR	% equity funding	Acquisition EV/EBITDA
10.0%	50.4%	37.0%	18.9%	6.9x
15.0%	41.4%	32.0%	21.8%	7.1x
20.0%	34.2%	28.0%	24.6%	7.4x
25.0%	28.3%	24.6%	27.2%	7.7x
30.0%	23.4%	21.6%	29.6%	7.9x
35.0%	19.1%	19.1%	31.9%	8.2x
40.0%	15.3%	16.8%	34.0%	8.5x

7. RECENT DEVELOPMENTS IN THE LBO MARKET

Increasing influence of private equity investors and falling returns

Private equity investors are becoming an increasingly dominant force in the M&A market. Over $200bn was raised by US private equity funds alone in 2006. A greater amount of funds mean more competition for assets and lower returns for private equity investors. In the early 1990s hurdle rate returns approximated 30%; these dropped to 25% by the late 1990s and now stand at around 20% for normal industrial company deals. In the infrastructure sector, returns can be even lower (sometimes as low as 12%).

A benign debt environment

Over the last seven years debt investors are increasing the leverage they will extend in private equity deals. Average total debt to EBITDA multiples were 5.8x EBITDA in the third quarter of 2006 (Financial Times 3/10/06). There are two drivers of increasing leverage.

- First, the profile of debt investors has changed from being mostly commercial banks and some high yield investors to hedge funds.
- Second, investors are increasingly willing to accept refinancing risk in the structure. For example the French yellow pages deal saw a bullet repayment Term A loan.

Staple finance

In competitive auctions, financial advisors (the investment banks) are increasingly packaging a business for sale combined with a debt financing facility. The debt facility is effectively "stapled" to the information memorandum of the business for sale. Stapled finance has the effect of:

- Speeding up the sale process, and underpinning the sale price by confirming an initial debt capacity
- Commoditizing the private equity forcing a competition among the bidders to see who will accept the lowest returns